COLUSA COUNTY FREE LIBRARY
3 0738 00146 5938

D0531913

FWD Corporation

". . . the truck was an emergency expedient to pull us out of a bad transportation hole in World War I (even then you couldn't kill it quite as easily as a horse); today's commercial vehicle has become an economic necessity to a nation whose entire life it has revolutionized."

A. F. Denham, 1942

BEKINS
PIANO
MOVING
Los Angeles, Cal.
Santa Fe

(Opposite page) Western Trucking Magazine

Automobile Manufacturers Association, Inc.

THIS WAS TRUCKING

A Pictorial History of the First Quarter Century of Commercial Motor Vehicles

By Robert F. Karolevitz.

SUPERIOR PUBLISHING COMPANY
Seattle, Washington

LIBRARY OF CONGRESS CARD CATALOGUE NUMBER 66-25421

FIRST EDITION

PRINTED IN THE UNITED STATES OF AMERICA
BY THE FRAYN PRINTING COMPANY
SEATTLE

(Title page) The General Motors Truck Company was formed by consolidating the firms which manufactured the Reliance and Rapid trucks. This pennant-bedecked Reliance thus was a forerunner of later GMCs. (Opposite title page) In 1903 Bekins Van & Storage Company introduced motorized hauling to the West Coast with this crude tiller-guided truck.

Los Angeles County Museum of History

In 1905 citizens of Los Angeles were startled to see this cumbersome Sturgis truck bring a new mode of transportation to Southern California. It was built locally for W. H. Manchester, who operated a freight and express service between Pomona and Los Angeles. Steering this archaic monstrosity required the brawn of a mule-skinner.

Dedication

LOOKING BACK, it is easy to conjure a romantic nostalgia about the early days of trucking. But for the men who built, drove, tested, financed and cussed the first unwieldy motor wagons, there was little glamour involved.

While the new-fangled automobiles were capturing the public fancy after the turn of the century, the commercial vehicles of the day faced tougher resistance. The automobile, in the beginning, was strictly a pleasure car. The truck, however, had to prove itself in dollars and cents.

Still, there were men who believed! Max Grabowsky, C. A. Tilt, the five Mack brothers, Otto Zachow, William Besserdich, Thomas B. Jeffery, Walter C. White, Captain A. E. Williams and others like them persisted against great odds and lukewarm sympathies.

Then, too, there were hundreds of unknown mechanics, teamsters, investors, promoters, inventors and just plain tinkerers who contributed bits and pieces to the total story. And certainly not to be overlooked were the draymen, merchants and other former users of horses who were willing to take a chance on something new!

To these pioneers who brought about a revolution in transportation, this book is respectfully dedicated.

HARDWARE

(Opposite page) Historical Collection, Title Insurance and Trust Company, San Diego

Harrah's Automobile Collection, Reno, Nevada

A Foreword

THE STORY OF TRANSPORTATION—from the earliest ages to the present day—has always been a fascinating one. The man-borne A-frame, the travois and the first crude wheel each marked milestones in an ever-changing saga.

Then, during the first quarter of the twentieth century, a most significant chapter in this continuing drama was written on converted wagon trails and rutted by-ways. While the spotlight of that day was ever on the revolutionary new motor cars, an equally revolutionary change was taking place in the technique of transporting goods.

The efforts of Duryea, Ford and the other master mechanics of their age were forcing the retirement of the high-stepping prancers which pulled the surreys with the fringe on top. At the same time they were dooming to pasture the gallant old dray horses which literally turned the wheels of commerce.

The purpose of this book is to focus a small measure of attention upon the early-day trucks which pioneered the motorized movement of beer kegs, cakes of ice and the countless products of a blossoming economy. They were hardly as at-

(Above) For three decades — beginning in 1900 — the Peerless Motor Car Company of Cleveland produced quality automobiles. Less known were the Peerless trucks such as this open-cab model with righthand drive. (Opposite page) Looking like a prop from a Mack Sennett silent movie, this ancient White trundled about the streets of Pomona, California, prior to World War I.

tractive as the Stutz Bearcats, the Stanley Steamers and the Thomas Flyers; yet, they were—in their own way—the rugged, romantic predecessors of the super-efficient highway leviathans which were to follow in later years.

As the story unfolds, it is obvious that several historical circumstances accelerated the development and the acceptance of motor trucks. Included were the Federal Road Act of 1916 and the emergency demands of World War I. The release of thousands of war-surplus vehicles after the Armistice further emphasized the demise of the horse as a factor in commercial transportation.

This book, as the sub-title indicates, is a pictorial history and, as such, does not attempt to report in great detail the successes and failures of individual truck manufacturers. That would, in fact, be a virtual impossibility because more than 300 companies came and went before 1925. Neither does this volume attempt to offer such technical details as torque, bore size, gear ratios or wheel base dimensions.

It is, instead, a graphic reminiscence of the transition from horses to horsepower on our nation's highways. The major goal has been to preserve in print the vintage photos of an industry which was too busy making history to worry about its archives. To this end, a diligent search was made of museums, libraries, newspaper morgues, company files and personal memorabilia. Already much valuable research material relating to this subject has been destroyed. It is our hope that this book will serve as a catalyst to cause those who still possess records and pictures of this remarkable era to attach to them the historical significance they deserve.

ROBERT F. KAROLEVITZ

The trucking industry started in the United States with small delivery vans. In the first decade of the twentieth century they came in every conceivable shape and size. They were powered by steam, electricity, gas and even by compressed air. They were the first to prove that motorized transport could be productive and profitable.

Zellerbach Paper Company

The Henry Ford Museum, Dearborn, Michigan

Automotive genius Henry Ford posed in 1917 with one of the trucks bearing his name. The first Ford truck was introduced in 1904. It was a small delivery wagon on a Model C chassis, having a capacity of 1,000 pounds and selling for $950. The first Model T truck was a 1911 delivery car priced at $750.

Acknowledgments

THIS ILLUSTRATED SAGA of the first quarter century of the trucking industry has been made possible because of an unusual cooperative effort. Pictorial histories depend upon the sleuthing job done by librarians, museum archivists, pioneers of the industry, public relations men, friends of the author and interested bystanders.

Without a representative collection of vintage photos, a volume of this type cannot hope to recreate the nostalgic atmosphere of another era. That is why I am particularly grateful to all those who have searched through aging files, long-forgotten albums, attics, trunks and other caches of memorabilia in behalf of this book. Their discoveries have helped me immensely in recording graphically the story of motorized transportation in its earliest years.

Specifically, I am appreciative of the cooperation extended me by the American Trucking Associations, Inc., the Automobile Manufacturers Association, Inc., the various truck companies, Harrah's Antique Automobile Collection, libraries, museums, highway departments and other allied organizations and trucking suppliers.

Staff members of the Seattle Public Library and the libraries of *The Seattle Times* and *The Seattle Post-Intelligencer* were especially helpful; so, too, were Robert D. Monroe, director of Special Collections, Suzzallo Library, University of Washington, and Kent Powell, editor and general manager of *Western Trucking Magazine*. Friends James W. Phillips and Ed Snyder provided continuing good counsel.

Once again, I am indebted to William O.

Thorniley for bringing vintage charm to the book with his antique type collection; to Emmet F. Billings for artistic touches where they were needed; and, of course, to my wife, Phyllis, who pounded out reams of correspondence, prepared the final manuscript and kept the coffee pot brewing.

The list below consists of my personal "honor roll" of those who contributed, in one way or another, to this project. To them (and any I might have overlooked through inadvertence), I repeat a sincere "thank you."

Those who helped...

Ray Beauchamp, *Seattle, Washington*
Jay Becker, *Seattle Chamber of Commerce*
E. P. Beezer, *Kenworth Motor Truck Company*
Walter W. Belson, *American Trucking Associations, Inc.*
Kenneth L. Bennett, *Fall City, Washington*
Donald Bogard, *Kent, Washington*
Larry Booth, *Title Insurance and Trust Company, San Diego*
Edward J. Boucher, *Michigan State Highway Department*
Pamela Brooke, *American Road Builders' Association*
Stanley K. Brown, *Colorado Department of Highways*
Mrs. Dale Bruget, *Yankton (S.D.) Press and Dakotan*
John A. Castle, *GMC Truck & Coach Division*
Roy F. Cauley, *Nevada Department of Highways*
Chester Chatfield, *The Boeing Company*
Henry Austin Clark, Jr., *Long Island (N.Y.) Automotive Museum*
Albert W. Coates, Jr., *Virginia Department of Highways*
Peter Craigmoe, *Union Oil Company of California*
Miss Kendall J. Cram, *Tennessee State Library and Archives*
Virginia Daiker, *The Library of Congress*
Arthur Danley, *FWD Corporation*
Raymond B. Dasch, *New Jersey State Highway Department*
John Deitrick, *Allied Public Relations, Inc. (for Mack Trucks, Inc.)*
John J. Dierbeck, Jr., *International Harvester Company*
William Dugovich, *Washington State Highway Department*
John J. Earley, *Oregon State Highway Department*
Henry E. Edmunds, *Director, Ford Archives*
Col. Virgil F. Field (AUS, Ret.), *Washington State National Guard*
Walter G. Fitzsimons, *Seattle, Washington*
C. P. Fox, *Circus World Museum*
Vernon R. Fry, *Carnation, Washington*
Mrs. Gail M. Gibson, *Pennsylvania Historical and Museum Commission*
T. W. Glaze, *Swift & Company*
Mike Goodrich, *Lansing Division, White Motor Corporation*
Gene M. Gressley, *Western History Research Center, University of Wyoming Library*
Glen R. Gulick, *Harrah's Automobile Collection, Reno, Nevada*
Loyal N. Gunderson, *Mission Hill, South Dakota*
George Gunn, Jr., *Seattle, Washington*
John F. Halloran, *North Dakota State Highway Department*
Robert C. Hare, *Carnation Company*
William Harper, *Seattle Historical Society Library*
Mrs. Elizabeth Hilderbrand, *Peoria (Ill.) Public Library*
Keith R. Hundley, *North Carolina State Highway Commission*
Ernest C. Jenner, *Seattle, Washington*
David V. Johnson, *White Motor Corporation*
Frank B. Karolevitz, *Salem, Oregon*
Lt. Raymond H. Kirlin, *Seattle Fire Department*
Charles F. Klamm, *State Highway Commission of Kansas*
Del Klaus, *Idaho Department of Highways*
Richard G. Knox, *Portland Cement Association*
Robert H. Loy, *The Indiana Motor Truck Association, Inc.*
Miss D. Lyman, *Vermont Department of Highways*
K. E. McCullum, *Texaco, Incorporated*
J. E. McGillicuddy, *LeTourneau-Westinghouse Company*
Larry Miller, *Automobile Manufacturers Association, Inc.*
Mrs. Jessie O'Connor, *Title Insurance and Trust Company, Los Angeles*
M. D. Poole, *Fraser Valley (B.C.) Milk Producers Association*
Neal R. Rew, *New York Department of Public Works*
Thomas G. Riley, *The Kelly-Springfield Tire Company*
Miss Elizabeth Ring, *Maine Historical Society*
Mrs. Carl Roediger, *Auglaize County (Ohio) Public Library*
William L. Rollins, *New Hampshire Department of Public Works and Highways*
Mrs. Ferne D. Roseman, *Indiana State Library*
John S. Rountree, *Standard Oil Company of California*
Clyde E. Schetter, *The Goodyear Tire & Rubber Company*
Francine Seders, *The Washington State Historical Society*
Henry R. Seidel, *Washington, D. C.*
Miss Jean Sonnhalter, *The Firestone Tire & Rubber Company*
Norwood Teague, *Los Angeles County Museum*
Henry A. Thomas, *Seattle, Washington*
Scott Wallace, *Carnation, Washington*
Arthur C. Waller, *Seattle, Washington*
Leonard Westrate, *Chevrolet Motor Division, General Motors Corporation*
H. S. Wiley, *New Mexico State Highway Commission*
Guy Williams, *Seattle, Washington*
Jerrold B. Winther, *Kenosha, Wisconsin*
Martin P. Winther, *Clermont, Florida*
Irwin W. Zeiger, *Central Motor Freight Association, Chicago*

(Left) Like many other manufacturers of automobiles, Chevrolet entered the truck field during the World War I era. This is a 1922 model with pneumatic tires, then becoming more and more popular. (Right) War-surplus Macks turned up in construction company and highway department fleets from one end of the U. S. to the other.

Chevrolet Motor Division, General Motors Corporation

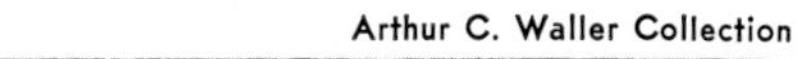

Arthur C. Waller Collection

Table of Contents

Once proven, trucks were put to work in every imaginable kind of job. Ford jitneys became cement batch trucks (top); rugged Whites hauled heavy equipment into the Wyoming oil fields; Reliance freight wagons rumbled along with gargantuan loads; in orchards and on country roads, motorized transport became an accepted reality.

Credits (top to bottom): Arthur C. Waller Collection; Western History Research Center, University of Wyoming; Automobile Manufacturers Association, Inc.; Pennsylvania Historical and Museum Commission, Harrisburg; Historical Collection, Title Insurance and Trust Company, San Diego.

SPENCERVILLE
BUILT
1875

(Opposite page) International Harvester Company

Smithsonian Institution

Crude, cumbersome steam vehicles were the forerunners of modern automobiles and trucks. In the U. S. such contraptions pre-date 1800 as Nathan Read of Salem, Massachusetts, and Apollo Kinsley of Hartford, Connecticut, operated steam devices during the decade 1790-1800. More than a half century later Richard Dudgeon of New York built the above "road wagon" which he drove successfuly for ten years before city officials reputedly banned it.

In the Very Beginning...

THE STORY OF THE GENESIS of motorized transportation has been told and re-told. Like other revolutionary and far-reaching achievements, the invention of self-propelled vehicles came about through an interminable process of trial and error, of success and failure, as hundreds of individuals—widely separated in time and geography—contributed bits and pieces to the ever-changing product.

It is little wonder that the saga leads down countless trails and byways, some to dead-ends of dejection and others to broad horizons of recognition and great wealth. Inevitably, such an expansive story must have its variations and controversies over minute details, but by and large, the highlights of this unending tale have been documented and recorded in the annals of transportation.

The idea of self-powered road devices goes back to antiquity. In 130 B.C., Hero of Alexandria predicted such an apparatus operated by steam. Homer mentioned "self-moved" contrivances in his immortal *Iliad.* The versatile genius, Leonardo da Vinci, was intrigued with the concept, and during the thirteenth century Roger Bacon wrote: "It will be possible to construct

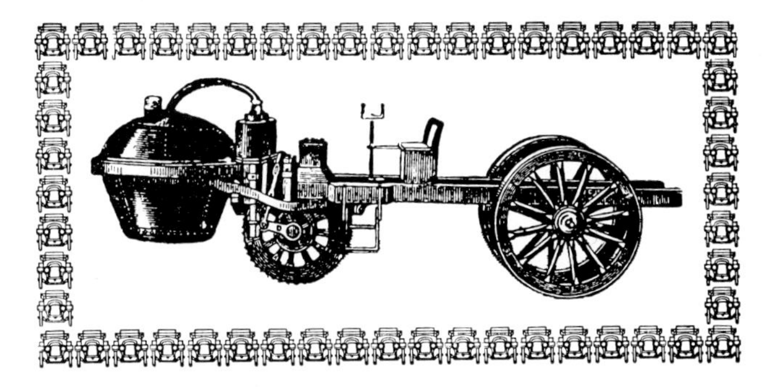

(Opposite page) Some of the earliest trucks were simply motorized versions of contemporary horse-drawn vehicles, like this 1907 International Auto Wagon. (Right) Captain Cugnot's ill-fated artillery tractor was not a success, but it spurred interest in steam-powered transportation.

chariots so that without animals they may be moved with incalculable speed."

As early as 1600 wind-driven carriages were operated in Holland. A century or more later, in Switzerland and in France, inventors tried to apply the principle of giant clock springs to carts and wagons.

Meanwhile, experimentation with the first crude engines was a harbinger of things to come. Compressed air, hydrogen gas, coal gas, ammonia, and steam were early sources of power as philosophers and mechanics combined forces in what became a relentless quest.

Finally in 1769, a French military officer—Capt. Nicholas Joseph Cugnot of Lorraine—designed a steam-propelled three-wheeled gun carriage which has come to be recognized as the first true ancestor of modern automobiles and trucks. Cugnot's device was not a practical success, however, though it achieved speeds of three miles an hour while carrying several passengers. In 1770 his second model overturned, destroyed a wall and Cugnot was imprisoned and then exiled.

But the race for perfection had begun. In England and on the Continent, men of vision worked unceasingly to overcome the deficiencies of huge steam boilers, ravenous fuel consumption and unsophisticated engineering. William Murdock, Richard Trevithick, William Symington, Sir Goldsworthy Gurney and Walter Hancock were among the leaders in England's Great Steam Era. The latter came to a stuttering halt in 1865 when a myopic Parliament passed the infamous Red Flag act. Steam-powered vehicles were not prohibited, but speeds on public roads were limited to two miles an hour in cities and twice that in the country. But more restrictive was the clause which required that every steam carriage have a crew of three, one of whom would precede the vehicle by not less than 60 yards carrying a red flag of warning. The effects of that ridiculous law stifled transportation progress in Great Britain for more than 30 years.

In France Charles Dallery of Amiens followed Cugnot's lead and constructed a successful steam

From top down: (1) Richard Trevithick, a Cornish mine captain, built his first steam-propelled road carriage in 1801 at Camborne, England. A second vehicle (shown here) was unveiled two years later and had driving wheels ten feet high. (2) Steam coaches designed by Sir Goldsworthy Gurney in the mid-1820s were unusually successful. They operated as a regular service between Gloucester and Cheltenham—a distance of nine miles—four times daily. (3) In 1833 F. Church added springs to the front wheel of his mammoth steam stage. (4) Frenchman Amédée Bollée-Pére, constructed this coal-fired carriage in 1872-73.

Historical Collection, Title Insurance and Trust Company, San Diego

The turn of the century brought great excitement to the field of land transportation. It marked the beginning of a nation-wide transition from bikes and buggies to motor cars and power wagons. Cycle shops and farm implement companies acquired automobile and truck agencies, and forward-thinking blacksmiths started to learn about engines and transmissions. In San Diego the Cycle & Arms Company (above) alertly added autos to its line.

carriage in 1790. By the turn of the century steam omnibuses were appearing regularly on the streets of Paris. At the same time Nathan Read of Salem, Massachusetts, and Apollo Kinsley of Hartford, Connecticut, unveiled steam vehicles to awe-struck spectators in the infant United States.

While the exponents of steam power were to persist for more than a century, another widely scattered group of inventors and mechanics was pursuing a totally different concept: the internal combustion engine. Again the historical chronology becomes difficult to trace, while claims and counter-claims have been commonplace through the years.

Carl Benz and Gottlieb Daimler, contemporary Germans who supposedly never met, are generally conceded pre-eminence in the field of gasoline-driven vehicles. Benz introduced his first car, a tricycle-type, in 1885, a year before Daimler completed a four-wheel model. Still earlier, however, were J. J. E. Lenoir, a Belgian, and Siegfried Marcus of Austria, who built workable autocarts in the 1860s.

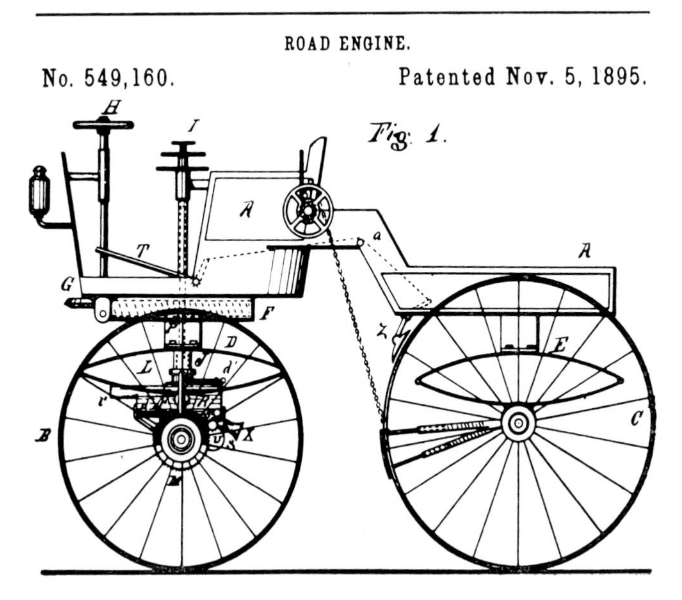

The famous Selden Patent brought much consternation and litigation to the infant automobile industry. In 1879 George Baldwin Selden of Rochester, New York, drew up specifications for a motor car which resulted in a valid patent 16 years later. Not until 1911 did the U. S. Court of Appeals abolish the royalty payments which greatly restricted early manufacturers.

Western Trucking Magazine

Ransom E. Olds was experimenting with steam vehicles as early as 1886, and his famous "curved dash runabout" which he introduced in 1901 was America's first really low-priced car. Two years later he sold his interest in the Olds Motor Works and then organized the Reo Motor Car Company. The latter firm produced this 1913 Reo Democrat Wagon, pictured here with Clarence A. Garrett of Garrett Freightlines, Inc., Pocatello, Idaho.

In the United States Charles E. and J. Frank Duryea teamed up to produce what is now considered to be the first successful gasoline-engine vehicle in America. It was first operated on September 21, 1893, in Springfield, Massachusetts, and consisted of a second-hand carriage (which the Duryeas bought for $70) and a one-cylinder engine.

The 1890s fairly bubbled with inventive activity as the race was on to reap the honors and financial rewards which were sure to come with the commercialization of "automobiles," a name which had not yet been universally attached to the wide variation in vehicles. The decade also brought U. S. Patent No. 549,160, an instrument of controversy which was to keep the new industry astir for 16 years.

In 1879 George Baldwin Selden, a perceptive young patent attorney in Rochester, New York, was so impressed with a two-cycle internal combustion motor designed by George B. Brayton that he proceeded to adapt it—on paper only—

(Left) Max Grabowsky of Detroit started building trucks in 1900 and two years later he established the Grabowsky Motor Vehicle Company to produce and sell this first model. In 1904 his firm's name was changed to the Rapid Motor Vehicle Company, after which it became part of the General Motors Truck Company. (Right) The W. N. Brockway Carriage Works, Inc., manufactured wagons and buggies in Homer, New York, before George A. Brockway, son of the founder, introduced a truck bearing the family name.

Truck and Coach Division, General Motors Corporation

Brockway Motor Trucks

In 1857 when he was 21 years old, Thomas H. White was working in a Massachusetts chair factory for $1.25 a day. In his spare time, however, he tinkered with an idea for a sewing machine, and two years later he was granted patents on his invention of a small hand-operated model with a single thread stitch. During the Civil War he built sewing machines in Orange, Massachusetts, and in 1866 moved to Cleveland, Ohio, to give himself a "broader territory." The White Sewing Machine Company prospered, and in 1894 it was ready to diversify. Soon the factory was turning out 10,000 bicycles a year. About this time Thomas White's three sons began to take an active part in the business. Windsor T., a graduate of Worcester Polytechnic Institute in 1890; Rollin H., who received an engineering degree from Cornell in 1893, and Walter C., a law graduate from the latter school in 1898, were all interested in the new horseless carriage craze, a fact which was to revolutionize the family business. Rollin invented a flash boiler for steam cars, and in 1900 the first White truck was built.

White Motor Corporation

to an idea for a "road engine." On May 8 of that year he filed his drawings with the U. S. Patent Office.

Sixteen years later—in 1895—the application was favorably approved and until 1911 almost every manufacturer of gasoline-propelled vehicles had to pay royalties to the holder of the Selden patent.

Everywhere, though, the interest in "horseless carriages" was growing to fever pitch. The emphasis, seemingly, was upon the production of pleasure cars—but at the same time activity was mounting in the field of commercial vehicles.

Just who was "first" in the flurry of experimentation which began in the mid-1890s is a moot consideration. Mechanics and inventors

Rugged steel-wheeled Kenworths came into being at a time when dozens of other makes were fading out of existence. The Kenworth cognomen was coined from the names of two of the firm's initial stockholders: E. K. Worthington and H. W. Kent. It was 1927 before the company produced more than 100 KWs in a single year.

Kenworth Motor Truck Company

FWD Corporation

(Above) The four-wheel-drive principle became a reality in 1908 when this kerosene-fired, steam-driven auto was tested in the snows of Clintonville, Wisconsin. Blacksmiths and brothers-in-law, Otto Zachow (left) and William A. Besserdich, at the controls, developed what was to become the FWD truck. (Below) In 1900 James Ward Packard organized the New York and Ohio Automobile Company. Three years later it moved to Detroit and became the Packard Motor Company, one of the earliest pioneers of both automobile and truck manufacturing. Note the distinctive Packard radiator and the righthand drive.

Automobile Manufacturers Association, Inc.

from coast to coast turned from bicycles and horse carriages to the new auto craze.

The Langert Company of Philadelphia entered a gasoline delivery wagon in the 1896 Cosmopolitan race (from New York City to Irvington-on-the-Hudson and return). In that same year the Cruickshank Engineering Works of Providence, Rhode Island, converted a horse van into a steam wagon for a local department store.

Farther west, Charles E. Woods, a Chicago carriage builder, was reputedly the first to produce work vehicles commercially with the introduction of several light electric delivery wagons. In Portland, Oregon, C. S. Fairfield built a sightseeing stage powered by a kerosene engine.

In 1898 the first vestiges of competition began to develop. Alexander Winton unveiled a tiller-guided gasoline delivery wagon, said to be the first such model produced in commercial quantities. Concurrently, the Duryea Motor Wagon Company of Springfield, Massachusetts, mounted a panel body on a three-wheel chassis. Meanwhile, A. L. Riker, a Columbia College Law School graduate more interested in electricity, was working feverishly on several battery-powered vehicles. In the 1898 electrical show held in Madison Square Garden, he exhibited a 2,900-

Lansing Division, White Motor Corporation

C. A. Tilt had been building Diamond T automobiles for six years before a customer asked him to produce this truck in 1911. It was so successful that Tilt stopped making passenger cars entirely. Tilt's father was a shoe manufacturer who used as a trademark a diamond for quality and a T for Tilt, a symbol later adopted for trucks and autos.

pound delivery wagon built for the B. Altman & Company dry goods store. The battery alone weighed 1,000 pounds!

It was an exciting head-over-heels era as hopeful manufacturers vied for acceptance by a skeptical public. Would the ultimate power be steam, gasoline, electricity or kerosene?

The Stanley brothers of Newton, Massachusetts, photographic dry-plate makers, entered the field with light steam delivery trucks. By 1900 the White Sewing Machine Company of Cleveland, Ohio, had a similar steam vehicle.

In 1899 the St. Louis Carriage Company introduced a small gasoline model with a piano-box body carrying the unique name, Rigs-that-Run. Waverleys, General Electrics, Columbias, Woods and Rikers were prominent battery-driven entries. With Samuel Insull as president, the Woods Motor Vehicle Company of Chicago sold several mail-collecting wagons to the U. S. Post Office Department and three 1,500-pound electric utility trucks to the U. S. Signal Corps.

Before the turn of the century, the threshold had been crossed. Private industry was obviously interested. The federal government was intrigued. The end of the beginning had come!

Mack Trucks, Inc.

This gas-operated sightseeing bus introduced a famous name to the field of automotive manufacturing. It was built in 1900 by the Mack Brothers in their Brooklyn wagon shop after they had experimented earlier with both steam and electric vehicles.

Pennsylvania Historical and Museum Commission, Harrisburg

One of the largest users of electric vehicles was the American Railway Express Company. This fleet of Commercial trucks was assembled for a photo in 1922. Electrics were particularly adaptable to the start-and-stop requirements of city delivery service. Extremely heavy batteries were a major drawback of these trucks.

The Electrics Were Something Special

THE SILENT, fumeless electric trucks of the early 1900s were unusual vehicles. Economical and relatively uncomplicated, they promised a great future which never quite materialized.

Before the turn of the century, the first electric delivery trucks were scooting around several of the larger eastern cities, proving remarkably effective (until their batteries ran down). Had there been no demand for inter-city transportation, the electrics may well have reigned supreme. Unfortunately, the availability of long-haul assignments caused the industry to emphasize the development of gasoline-powered trucks, while steamers and battery-driven vehicles got secondary attention.

As early as 1838 Robert Davidson of Aberdeen, Scotland, built a crude electric road machine, but not until the 1880s was any concerted effort de-

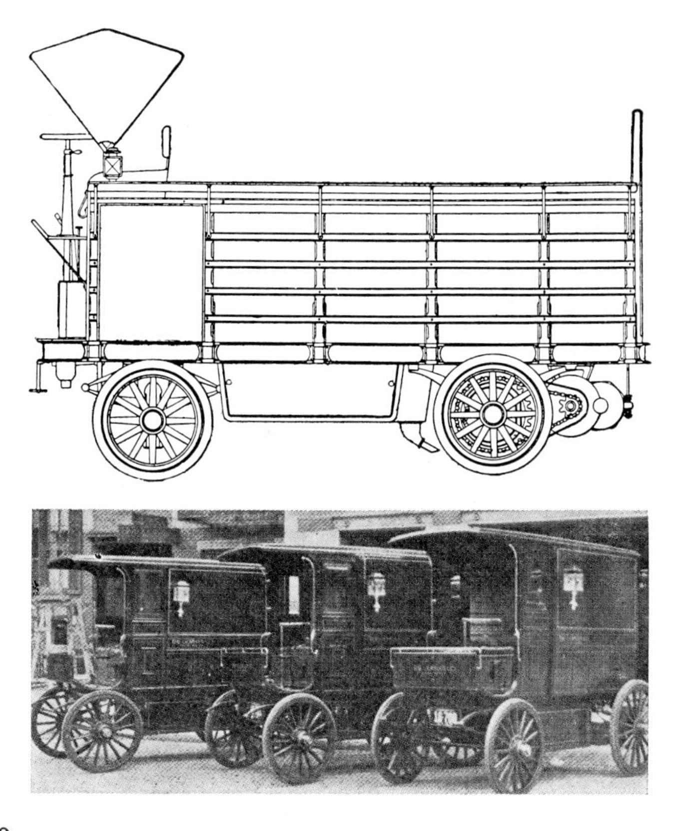

(Top right) This drawing shows the unusual chain-drive arrangement used on some of the heavier early-day electric trucks, the power unit being suspended behind the rear wheels. (Bottom right) The chassis of a Commercial Truck Company electric, the same make as those shown in the fleet above.

voted to this form of automotive power. Then, in 1881, M. Rafford of France introduced an electric carriage. A year later a battery-powered tricycle was developed in Great Britain. But it took the Immisch Electric Company of Kentish Town, England, to attract international attention when it converted a four-wheel dog cart into a chain-driven electric car which it sold to the Sultan of Turkey. He was so pleased with his unique conveyance that he bought another to be delivered in 1890.

Meanwhile, Fred M. Kimball & Company of Boston produced the first practical electric automobile in the United States, delivering it to P. W. Pratt in 1888, five years before the Duryeas brought out their original gas model. In 1890 A. L. Riker, one of the most important of the early trucking pioneers, built an operable electric car. Seven years later he unveiled the first successful battery-driven truck produced in America.

From the beginning, electric trucks were limited by their batteries. While gasoline vehicles could be refueled almost anywhere—by a can and funnel, if necessary—the electrics normally had to return to their garage for recharging. Consequently, they were known in the industry as "homing pigeons." Their radius of operation was governed by the staying power of their batteries, and, like Cinderella, they had to race for home before the last spark of electro-chemical magic faded away.

The first lead batteries were heavy and unwieldy. By 1908 Thomas Alva Edison—a great exponent of electric vehicles—improved on that problem with a new iron-nickel-alkaline battery. Still, the basic difficulty—the inability to be refueled on the road—was to be a continual and vital deterrent to the ultimate success of the electric truck.

There was also another problem.

Batteries made no noise. They didn't vibrate. Because their operation was electro-chemical in nature, they were little understood by the men who had to use them. Consequently, with no symptoms to indicate trouble, batteries were often ill-used through ignorance by teamsters and stablemen who had switched (by necessity) from horses and probably weren't too happy about it.

The most extensive users of electric trucks—department stores, bakeries, laundries, express companies, etc.—recognized the drawbacks and compromised in order to claim the obvious advantages. They planned routes to match the longevity of the power output. They developed efficient charging equipment and purchased extra batteries—so that one set could be on the job while another was being revitalized.

For this they received an economically operated delivery truck, one which lasted three or more times longer than a gasoline model and required considerably less maintenance (an electric truck had 1,000 fewer operating parts).

Unfortunately, the advantages were not enough, and by 1925 electric vehicles were gradually disappearing from the commercial scene.

There are those who say, however, that—unlike the horse—the electric truck will stage a comeback!

During their hey-day, electric trucks came in a wide variety of shapes and sizes. All were characterized, however, by the battery storage compartment or "cradle" beneath the chassis.

PETROLEUM
PRODUCTS
THE TEXAS COMPANY
PETROLEUM
PRODUCTS
THE TEXAS COMPANY

(Opposite page) Public Relations Archives, Texaco, Inc.

American Trucking Associations, Inc.

(Above) A soon-to-be-replaced dray horse stared quizzically at his new rival, a Consolidated motor truck, being tested in 1904 by the American Express Company. (Below) This prophetic cartoon by Homer Davenport appeared in the *New York Journal* in 1899.

Old Dobbin's Last Stand

No one knows when man first domesticated the horse. But as long as there has been recorded history — scrawled on walls of caves, Egyptian obelisks or papyrus-reed paper—evidences of this faithful beast of burden appear time and time again.

For more than 4,000 years the horse has carried cavalry into war, pulled the chariots of turbaned rulers and raced for the laurels of victory along the Nile, the Euphrates and over the plains of ancient Cathay.

In the beginning, the horse was not used for the mundane toils of agriculture and drayage; the ass and the oxen filled that servile niche. Gradually, though, as the "great horses" of Northern Europe and the British Isles were developed, a new "work" role evolved.

Over a span of four score centuries gallant steeds contributed to the advance of civilization.

(Opposite page) Gallant old hay-burners continued to serve the petroleum industry until well after World War I. In Port Arthur, Texas, this team was doggedly holding on in the face of stiff competition from 3½-ton "Bulldog" Macks.

Washington Trucking Magazine

This turn-of-the-century picture taken in San Francisco showed the need of three-horse teams for moving vans. Decriers of Old Dobbin preached inefficiency, high costs and just plain messiness. The two motor bikes in the scene were harbingers of things to come as self-propelled vehicles inevitably grew more numerous.

They were honored in statues of stone and of bronze, on coins, medallions and magnificent murals. Their contributions on the battlefield, in Olympiad competition and in the exploration of the New World were lauded by poet and historian.

Then, almost overnight, the horse suddenly became Old Dobbin, and he found himself cast as the antithesis of progress!

The villain, of course, was the self-powered vehicle—the chariot, the buggy, the wagonette which needed no horse for motivation.

They say change comes slowly, but for the horse the reversal came like a lightning bolt against the backdrop of history. One day he was King of the Road; on the next, advertising writers were decrying his inability to produce, his expense of upkeep, his "old-fashionedness."

When strange "autocars" originally began to sputter on cobblestone streets and country lanes, public opinion was in Old Dobbin's corner. The first brave souls who experimented with gasoline and steam contraptions found little favor for harnessing evil power and befouling the air. Each run-away horse caused by a smoke-belching Winton, Haynes-Apperson or a Duryea "buggy-aut" brought forth a rain of abuse on the begoggled driver.

In the late 1890s, for instance, the people of South Dakota were virtually up-in-arms because of a home-made contrivance built by Louis Greenough and Harry Adams of Pierre. It consisted of a special Elkhart wagon powered by a two-cylinder Wolverine gasoline motor.

The machine worked and was capable of carrying up to eight passengers. Greenough and Adams hoped to get their investment back by charging for rides at county fairs. But the citizenry wasn't ready for such progress. At Mitchell they were refused permission to bring their vehicle inside the town limits. The Yankton *Press and Dakotan* warned editorially: "It is a dead moral certainty that the infernal machine

Seattle Post-Intelligencer Library

Unhurried old work horses were common sights on the streets of every city and hamlet in the United States. In 1912 there were 25,000,000 of them in the country. A year earlier, during a July heat wave, 1,200 horses dropped dead in the streets of New York City alone, a gruesome fact which truck publicists promoted at every turn.

will frighten horses and endanger the lives of men, women and children."

Almost as suddenly, however, an anti-horse sentiment began to develop. In the first issue of *The Automobile Magazine* in 1899 a writer named Sylvester Baxter lashed out thusly:

"It is peculiarly appropriate that some cold facts about the horse be laid before the public at the present time. These will substantiate the assertion that the horse is an animal of extraordinary little sense—using the word as synonymous with judgment. He has a remarkable delicate perception, coupled with a very slight power of correlation. He is therefore subject to seizure at any moment with fits of the most violent insanity, induced at the slightest provocation. This, together with the enormous reserve strength of the animal, makes him an exceedingly dangerous engine to be practically given the freedom of the road in our populous communities."

Baxter went on to tell about the terrible accidents, the slaughtered children and the maimed adults, all caused by that evil character, the horse. He then cited 476 case histories of runaways, and proudly announced that only two were caused by the sight of an automobile.

The same magazine editorially described the horse as "one of the greatest drags upon the wheels of progress." The writer continued:

"He is the chief maker of the vast and overwhelming din that envelops the modern city. It is for the horse that the stone pavements are laid, to keep his feet from slipping. And over every separate stone, set to that end, he drags bumpingly, poundingly, crashingly, with unceas-

Western Trucking Magazine

From 1903 to 1910 the entire truck production in the U. S. amounted to 10,374. Still, the transition from horses to motor vehicles was well underway. Many firms like Bekins made the change gradually, replacing a few teams at a time.

Washington State Department of Highways

Some of the romance went out of firefighting with the passing of horse-drawn equipment. However, the vivid excitement of flying hooves and clanking bells was not enough to combat the economics of the motor truck.

ing rattlety-bang, the endless procession of clamoring carriages, wagons, carts and drays. Then at the end of the day every frequented street that meanwhile has not been constantly cleaned is literally carpeted with a warm, brown matting of comminuted horse-dropping, smelling to heaven and destined in no inconsiderable part to be scattered in fine dust in all directions, laden with countless millions of disease-bearing germs."

Poor Old Dobbin!

He had never asked for all that work in the first place—and now he was being villified as a moronic quadruped, a purveyor of plague, a murderer of children and a noisy, loathsome barrier in the path of progress.

It was a strange turn of events. Automobile salesmen were arguing that a horseless city is a flyless city . . . a clean, quiet, odorless city. The automobile would make things right in the world!

Realistically, though, the last decade of the nineteenth century and the first 15 years of the twentieth constituted a period of transition from animal to automotive power—with each side having outspoken champions.

The raucous cry—"Get a Horse!"—resounded across the land, until it became obvious that the automobile was here to stay. All except the most obstinate die-hards finally conceded that pleasure cars would indeed replace buggies, surreys and the one-hoss shay.

But on the farm, for construction and for commercial hauling, the draft horse was equally ensconced in perpetuity. At least that was the general opinion as the new century began to unfold. Few individuals even remotely suspected

This San Diego fire chief trusted the new-fangled motor trucks for his hose and ladder equipment, but he very conservatively retained a white charger for his own use.

Seattle Fire Department

Motorized firefighting equipment unquestionably surpassed the horse-drawn kind for speed and capability—but when it came to a parade, a handsome team pulling a glittering steamer continued to be the greatest crowd-pleaser. This old-and-new combination appeared in the Potlatch Parade in Seattle, Washington, 1912.

the rapidity with which trucks and tractors would appear to challenge Old Dobbin's work capabilities. With each new automotive improvement, he lost more of his supporters. In the end he would be left only with sentimentalists, the most rabid reactionaries and one or two religious sects who stayed with the horse for reasons of their own.

In the end, the argument which was Old Dobbin's final undoing was an economic one. Bookkeepers, with green eyeshades and gartered sleeves, did more to drive the nation's dray horses to pasture than any of the sharp-penned advertising writers with their contrived "facts" and obvious bias.

The more astute operators—major department stores and express companies—began to make careful comparisons between the costs of truck and horse deliveries. Even the earliest such studies showed favorably for self-propelled vehicles, and as trucks got better, the advantages became more pronounced.

The penny-counters really prepared a case against Old Dobbin.

They drew up tables and graphs and assorted charts to spell out just how expensive horse

Historical Collection, Title Insurance and Trust Company, San Diego

(Top) Seattle Post-Intelligencer Library; (Center right) Historical Collection, Title Insurance and Trust Company, San Diego; (Center left and bottom) Union Oil Company of California

There was something paradoxical about horses delivering gas and oil for the motor vehicles which were about to replace them. In time the old tank wagons disappeared, and motorized units—like the Moreland (center left) and the "Bulldog" Mack (center right)—rightfully assumed the burgeoning task of petroleum supply.

transportation really was. The following pre-World War I tabulation was typical:

Cost of Operating One Horse and Wagon

	Per Month*
Horse Keep	$ 32.50
Shoeing	2.51
Wagon Repair	4.00
Harness Repair	.87
Total	(39.88)
Driver's Wages	60.00
Total	(99.88)
Depreciation, Horse	4.00
Depreciation, Wagon	3.00
Depreciation, Harness	1.67
Interest, Horse, 6%	1.20
Interest, Wagon, 6%	1.25
Interest, Harness, 6%	.40
Total	$111.20
Value of Horse (Life—5 Years)	$240.00
Value of Wagon (Life—7 Years)	250.00
Value of Harness (Life—2 Years)	40.00

*17 miles per day

With that table, the accountant documented that a horse-and-wagon cost a businessman $111.20 a month . . . or $4.45 a day . . . or more than 26 cents a mile.

But that didn't count a replacement horse, because one animal couldn't possibly travel 17 miles a day for 300 or more days a year.

When it was all said and done, trucks—traveling at the rate of 12 miles an hour 50 miles a day—could operate for at least ten cents a mile less. The more teams a company required, the more the costs pyramided.

Truly, the handwriting was in the ledger books and on the stable wall. Each new computation made the horse look worse—and this was the kind of message any businessman (no matter how sentimental) could understand. In the past he hadn't thought much about the fact that he had to feed his horses every day whether they worked or not. He little considered the expense of replacement teams, sick horses or fence-mend-

Old Dobbin was everywhere and replacing him was no simple over-night task. He hauled milk cans, ice cream and massive logs. He delivered beer kegs, hay bales, cobblestones and cascara bark. Express wagons, like those in front of Seattle's North West Hotel (bottom right) were vital to the commerce of the day.

Credits (top to bottom): Historical Collection, Title Insurance and Trust Company, San Diego; Indiana State Library; King County (Washington) Engineer; The Seattle Times.

Truck and Coach Division, General Motors Corporation

The New Dells Lumber Company of Eau Claire, Wisconsin, replaced 16 horses with one truck—and the General Motors Truck Company told the world about it.

ing. He took for granted the huge barns, the blacksmithing bills and the interminable pitching of hay.

What a businessman's bookkeeper didn't show him, representatives of the new truck companies did. Old Dobbin was just too expensive to have around, that's all . . . because he ate too much, he demanded too much space and attention, and he was woefully inefficient by comparison.

The object, of course, was to sell trucks. The horse, as a horse, was not a pariah—but as a business machine, he was a plodding target. By 1912 the "horse vs. truck" controversy was in full swing. The General Motors Truck Company editorialized in a late-spring publication:

"During the next three months it will be no unusual sight to see horses dropping dead on the streets, having succumbed to the heat. . . . The beauty of the motor truck is that it is not affected by the heat. It can go from early morning till late evening, and if conditions demand, it can be run all night and be ready for another day's work."

Later GMC got more graphic, issuing a full-page advertisement which showed ten different gruesome pictures of horses dying in the streets, surrounded by frantic drivers and the morbid curious.

In 1915 *The Chicago Tribune* got into the act with this commentary:

"Sanitation opposes the use of the horse, and in a great city, where congestion is chronic, the tremendous saving in celerity and space represented by the more compact and powerful motor vehicle is a most important consideration. The horse loses heavily in efficiency in bad weather, the motor little. This means that business is little disorganized and retarded when the motor is used."

The truck promoters lost no opportunities to lambast Old Dobbin. In spite of the fact that thousands of horses were dying on the battlefields of France, the anti-equine writers used World War I as the final blow in the sideline battle between automotive and animal power. One writer penned:

"Five acres of farm land are necessary to produce the food consumed each year by a single

In Tacoma, Washington, Little & Kennedy Company promoted Signal trucks by comparison with less efficient horse-drawn vehicles. Anti-horse themes were common in early-day truck advertising.

Washington State Historical Society

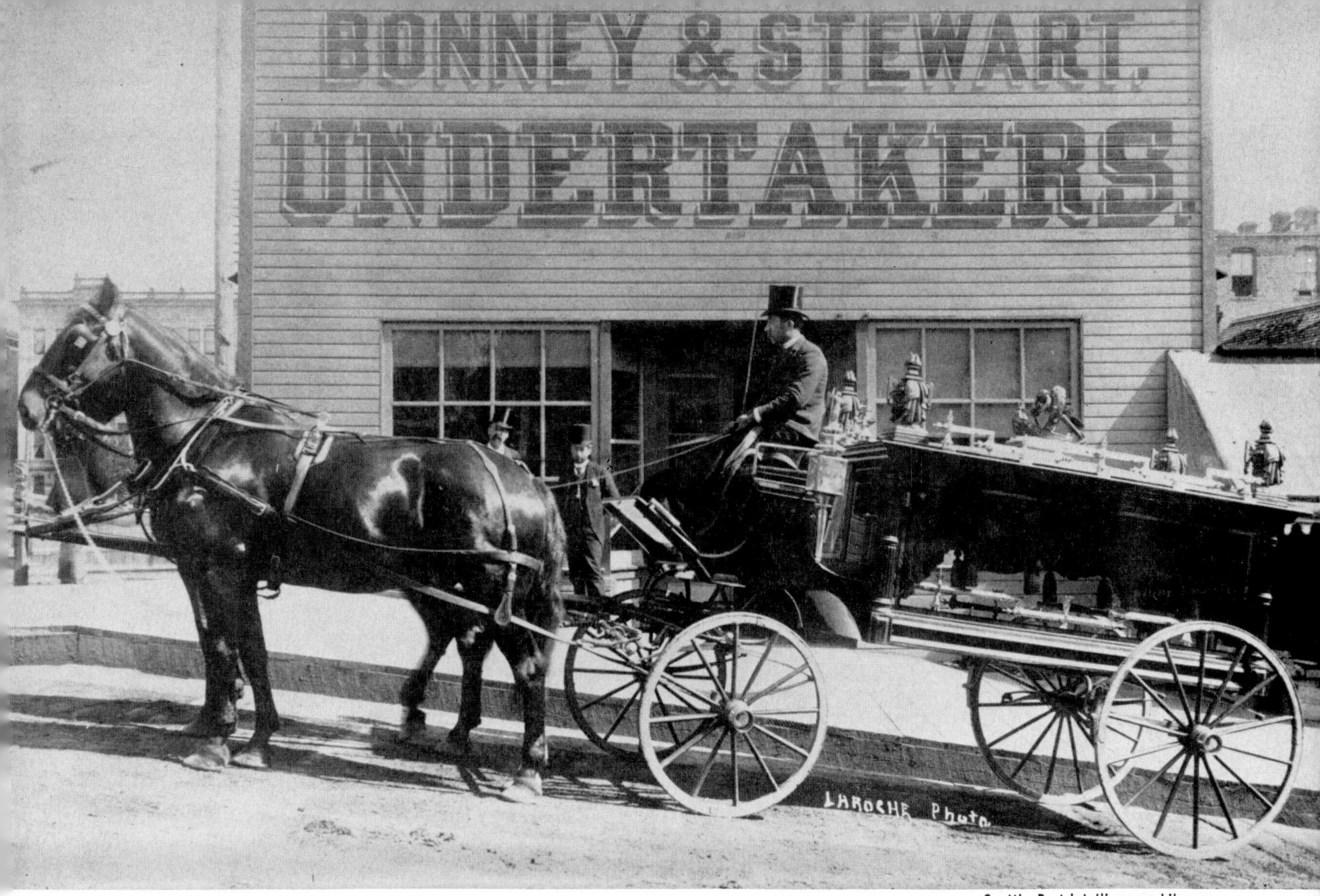

Seattle Post-Intelligencer Library

The jet-black steeds of the local mortician played their somber role with great dignity. They seemed to be more intimately involved in the solemnity of the occasion than the impersonal motor vehicles which sent them to pasture.

horse, who eats about 12,000 pounds annually. Based upon an estimated 24 million horses in the United States, the acreage devoted to keeping them alive is more than sufficient to feed the entire human population of the country."

He went on dramatically:

"It has been estimated that the iron used up on horseshoes every year would build 40,000 tractors or 60,000 motor cars, and that the leather needed for harnesses would be valued at approximately $150 million. Right now leather and iron are needed . . . for military purposes."

There it was, in black and white, Old Dobbin had become a virtual traitor to his country!

The passing of the horse as a factor in commerce was certainly not abrupt; as a matter of fact, he is still with us in a few specialized uses. But bow out he did—almost as rapidly as truck manufacturers could build vehicles to replace him. Interestingly enough, truck dealers across the land found themselves in the "used horse" business. To get potential customers to switch to trucks, they offered to take horses in trade. George Gunn, Jr., a youthful dealer in the logging fields of Western Washington, sold his first Kelly-Springfield and wound up with 18 horses in the bargain.

Gradually, the inevitable took place. Old Dobbin came out second best in the debate, and when peace was declared in Europe, the truck manufacturers found themselves in another and more

Vermont Department of Highways (U.S. Bureau of Public Roads)

Side by side, a war-surplus "Bulldog" Mack and a dejected-looking team await the loader in a Vermont gravel pit. For Old Dobbin, it was the beginning of the end!

Seattle Post-Intelligencer Library

Fourth of July parades in 1908 were gala affairs with a wide variety of participation. This gravity-type sprinkling wagon joined the festivities; then, undoubtedly, it went back over the parade route behind the street cleaners. While the emphasis in this chapter has been on horses, mules, too, were victims of the motor truck.

difficult competitive situation. Now they had to take on each other. Before, it was all for one against the horse. With their common "enemy" out of the race, they plunged into a perpetual truck-versus-truck battle.

Meanwhile, the horse slowly faded from the commercial scene. Some old-timers held out as long as possible, but the romantic old beer wagons, the dramatic excitement of fire horses answering an alarm and the village blacksmith with his flaming forge and ringing anvil all succumbed to progress.

Harness-making became a dying art. Words like "hame," "whiffletree" and "springhalt" virtually disappeared from the national vocabulary. In time, even the U. S. Army abandoned its once illustrious horse cavalry. And during its convention of 1940, the International Brotherhood of Teamsters dropped the word "Stablemen" from the union's official name.

The motor truck—in less than three decades—had revolutionized centuries-old transportation methods. As truck advocates were to learn, they were creating a few problems of their own, but in the pioneering days, boundless enthusiasm pervaded the industry. There was little time for negativism—except as it related to Old Dobbin and his uneconomical ways.

Horse-drawn hearses, water wagons and garbage vans were stored away. Livery stables be-

Automobiles and motorcycles were still the object of curiosity when this picture was taken in 1910. Horse-drawn tank wagons were commonplace in an era when water supply was a concern and street-cleaning a universal necessity.

The Seattle Times

Pennsylvania Historical and Museum Commission, Harrisburg

An early model Packard shared a Philadelphia street with horse-drawn wagons and carriages. The two modes of transportation created problems for one another during the long transition period, not the least of which was the defensive belligerence of the men who drove the horses.

came garages. Even Standard Oil, Texaco and other petroleum companies decided it was time to shift to tank trucks for gasoline deliveries. After all, there was a new corporate image to create! The horse was obsolete; the era of the motor truck had dawned, for better or for worse.

The United States Post Office Department was one of the first governmental agencies to turn to motorized transportation, experimenting with small collection trucks as early as 1899. Horse-carts (below) ultimately gave way to gas and electric models of various types.

(Below) The Seattle Times; (Right) Automobile Manufacturers Association, Inc.

Los Angeles Examiner
509
ZEROLENE
MORELAND
DISTILLATE TRUCK
THIS TRUCK INSURED BY ROYAL INSURANCE CO.
THE BEHRENDT LEVY CO. AGENTS. LOS ANGELES.
PACIFIC COAST DEPT. ROYAL INSURANCE BLDG S.F.
MORELAND DISTILLATE TRUCK
MORELAND Two Ton Distillate Truck; Loaded and Lubricated with ZEROLENE
THE STANDARD OIL FOR MOTOR CARS
Leaving The Los Angeles Examiner Office 4 p.m. MAY. 3. 1913 For San Francisco
Examiner Office and Returning to Los Angeles Examiner Office.

(Opposite page) Standard Oil Company of California

Automobile Manufacturers Association, Inc.

From 1905 to 1913 the annual Glidden Tour was a highlight of the automotive year. While most of the participating vehicles were pleasure cars, this Rapid Truck covered several trips as a baggage wagon.

Tests, Tears and Triumphs

WHEN AUTOMOBILES AND TRUCKS were in their infancy, there seemed to be an impelling urge on the part of owners and manufacturers to race, test and exhibit them.

Contests of speed, strength and endurance were considered the best possible opportunities to prove to the world that the motor vehicle—for pleasure and for commerce — was "here" *ad infinitum.*

The challenge of competition helped speed up the development of autos and trucks as inventors and builders vied with one another for innovations and improvements. A race was considered a good yardstick of a vehicle's capabilities; so was a long-distance run.

In 1895 *The Chicago Times-Herald* sponsored the first two automotive races ever held in the United States. On November 2 that year a four-car contest was attempted, only to have breakdowns and accidents eliminate all starters. Then, on November 28—Thanksgiving Day—four gas and two electric autos sputtered off on a 53½-mile junket from Chicago's Jackson Park to Evanston and back. A three-inch snowfall provided an unexpected complication and forced the electric entries out of the race early, even though they had ropes around their wheels for traction and freshly charged batteries cached along the way.

In the end, only two cars finished. J. Frank Duryea in a Duryea Motor Wagon chugged home

American Trucking Associations, Inc.

(Opposite page) A Moreland two-ton distillate truck made a record run from Los Angeles to San Francisco and back in 1913. Its total time was 58½ hours on the road. Proof of a truck's capabilities and valuable publicity were the factors behind such early-day tests. (Right) This Waterless Knox led all entries in the first commercial vehicle competition held in New York City in 1903.

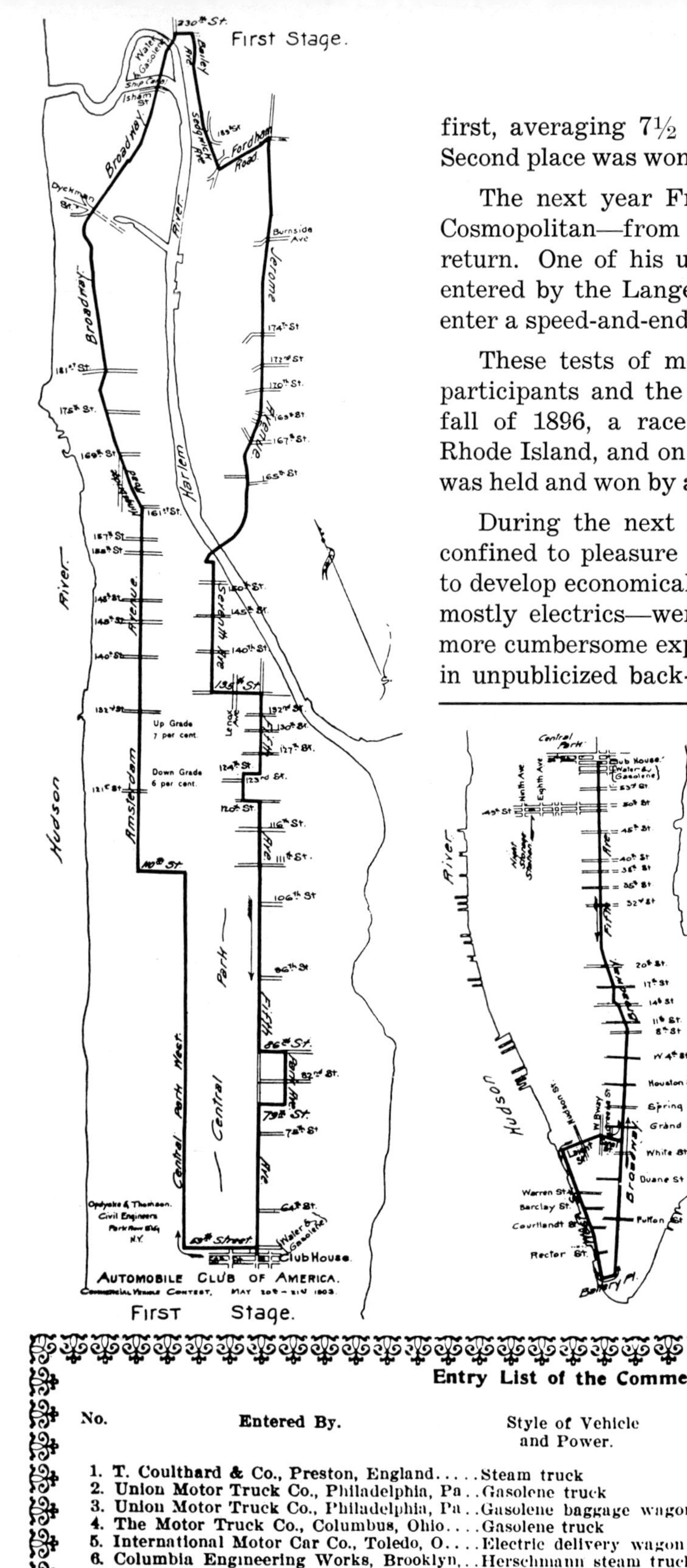

first, averaging 7½ miles an hour, not counting stops for repairs. Second place was won by an imported Mueller-Benz.

The next year Frank Duryea won the nation's third race—the Cosmopolitan—from New York City to Irvington-on-the-Hudson and return. One of his unsuccessful competitors was a delivery wagon, entered by the Langert Company of Philadelphia, the first truck to enter a speed-and-endurance contest.

These tests of men and machines were exciting events for the participants and the few spectators who heard about them. In the fall of 1896, a race track was established at Narraganset Park, Rhode Island, and on September 7 the first closed-course competition was held and won by a Riker Electric Stanhope.

During the next several years most of the racing activity was confined to pleasure cars, as truck manufacturers worked diligently to develop economically functional vehicles. Small delivery wagons—mostly electrics—were being tested "on the job," while builders of more cumbersome experimental steam trucks tried out their creations in unpublicized back-alley runs. Then, in 1903, the fledgling Auto-

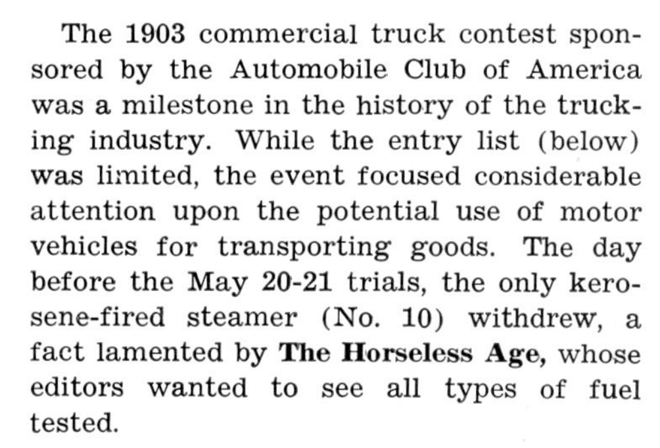

The 1903 commercial truck contest sponsored by the Automobile Club of America was a milestone in the history of the trucking industry. While the entry list (below) was limited, the event focused considerable attention upon the potential use of motor vehicles for transporting goods. The day before the May 20-21 trials, the only kerosene-fired steamer (No. 10) withdrew, a fact lamented by **The Horseless Age,** whose editors wanted to see all types of fuel tested.

The maps at the left show the routes laid out for the two-day competition. The first stage started at the A.C.A. clubhouse at Fifth Avenue and 58th Street in New York City. Both the delivery wagons and heavy trucks were required to make the 20-mile run to 230th Street and back on each of the two days. The second and third stages were identical ten-mile runs to the Battery and back, through streets considerably more congested.

Entry List of the Commercial Vehicle Test.

No.	Entered By.	Style of Vehicle and Power.	Allotted Class.	Character of Fuel	Rated H.-P.	Weight of Car Lbs.	Carrying Capacity Pounds	Kinds of Tires.
1.	T. Coulthard & Co., Preston, England	Steam truck	5th	Coke	30	12000	12000	Metal
2.	Union Motor Truck Co., Philadelphia, Pa	Gasolene truck	3d	——	20	5600	3500	Solid rubber
3.	Union Motor Truck Co., Philadelphia, Pa	Gasolene baggage wagon	3d	——	16	5400	3000	Solid rubber
4.	The Motor Truck Co., Columbus, Ohio	Gasolene truck	3d	——	10	4800	4000	Firestone
5.	International Motor Car Co., Toledo, O	Electric delivery wagon	1st	——	6	2100	1050	G. & J.
6.	Columbia Engineering Works, Brooklyn	Herschmann steam truck	5th	Coal	25	20000	10000	Solid rubber
7.	Columbia Engineering Works, Brooklyn	Herschmann steam truck	Miscel'ous	Coal	15	4800	2400	Solid rubber
8.	Grout Bros., Orange, Mass	Steam delivery wagon	2d	G. or K.	12	1800	2400	Diamond
9.	Morgan Motor Co., Worcester, Mass	Steam truck	4th	Coal	20	10700	6000	Metal
10.	Empire State Engineering Co., N. Y.	Steam delivery wagon	Miscel'ous	Kerosene	10	4800	2000	Hartford
11.	Knox Automobile Co., Springfield, Mass	Gasolene delivery wagon	2d	——	8	1900	1500	Diamond
12.	Knox Automobile Co., Springfield, Mass	Gasolene delivery wagon	2d	——	16	2200	2000	Dunlop
14.	Blaisdell & Co., Brooklyn, N. Y.	Steam delivery wagon	2d	Gasolene	10	3500	2000	Firestone
10.	Mobile Co. of America, N. Y	Steam delivery wagon	1st	Gasolene	4½	1500	750	Diamond

No. 10, relinquished by the Empire State Engineering Co., was awarded to the Mobile entry on Wednesday.

mobile Club of America decided to sponsor the first commercial vehicle contest in history.

The Horseless Age, first of the automotive trade publications in the United States, opined that "the motor must end its purely butterfly existence and be made to assume its share of the world's work, if it is to survive." The road test, it concluded, was the most logical way to answer the prosaic question: "Can the motor vehicle be made to pay?"

The 1903 contest was a most unusual event, and never before had such a strange conglomeration of vehicles been brought together. The entry list (on the opposite page) shows the wide variation in weight, power source and carrying capacity of the trucks involved.

The historical event was scheduled for two days—May 20-21—over a two-section course beginning at the A.C.A. clubhouse on Fifth Avenue. The entries were divided roughly into two classes: delivery wagons and heavy trucks, the former required to make a total run of 40 miles and the latter ten miles less on each of the two days.

Promptly at 9 a.m., on Wednesday, May 20, the six-ton coke-burning Coulthard from England chugged off on the 20-mile first stage leg of the test. Ten other entries followed at three minute intervals.

Unsuspecting New Yorkers along the course must have gawked in wonder at the strange procession of horseless wagons obviously engaged in some sort of race. As it turned out, the first day was unusually successful. Only one of the six delivery wagons—the Blaisdell—failed to finish when a hand pump broke and its gasoline supply caught fire. A leaky boiler sidelined No. 6, the massive Herschmann steamer which carried a 10,000-pound granite block.

Winner on the first day was No. 11, the Waterless Knox, a converted pickup-type pleasure car carrying 1,250 pounds of pig lead. With H. A. Knox at the controls, it covered the 40 miles in

A second commercial truck contest was held in 1904. One of the 18 starters was this gasoline model entered by Consolidated Motor Company. Carrying a ton-and-a-half load, it covered 239½ miles in a running time of 25.39 hours, one of the prize-winning efforts of the event. As clumsy as it looked, it was far superior to horse-drawn vehicles.

American Trucking Associations, Inc.

Automobile Manufacturers Association, Inc.

A Swiss-made Saurer accomplished the first transcontinental trip by motor truck in 1911. All sorts of obstacles were encountered during the historical trek, including a lack of proper railroad crossings. Note the 13-star flag.

the elapsed time of three hours and 35 minutes, using four gallons of gasoline. The second Herschmann, carrying a 3,805-pound load of cobblestones, led the heavy trucks in after six hours and 31 minutes on the road. Its fuel consumption for the 30 miles consisted of 230 pounds of hard coal and 172 gallons of water.

On the second day the trucks covered the same ground, but they were required to make a number of involuntary stops to simulate deliveries. Once more the Waterless Knox, its two-cylinder air-cooled engine unfazed by the 90-degree heat, romped home the winner. Its elapsed time on Thursday was just seven minutes longer than on the previous day. Again it was the No. 7 Herschmann which paced the heavy vehicles, cutting almost two hours off its first-day time.

The casualties on Thursday included No. 3, the Union baggage wagon, which threw a tire and overturned. The second Union entry, in the heavy-weight class, also failed to finish when the driver panicked on a hill and bent the engine shaft when he tried to stop a backward roll.

For the 80-mile total, the winning Knox used 10¼ gallons of gasoline. The Waverley electric used an estimated $2.50 in current for the same distance. The Herschmann express, in covering the allotted 60 miles for heavy trucks, burned up 410 pounds of coal and 332 gallons of water, while the mammoth Coulthard consumed 1,335 pounds of coke and 869 gallons of water.

The Horseless Age concluded after the event that delivery wagons had "arrived" but that heavy trucks were still in an embryonic stage. It also announced that solid rubber tires had it all over pneumatics and plain iron wheels for

Historical Collection, Title Insurance and Trust Company, San Diego

This painting depicts the difficulties of a cross-country run between Denver and Los Angeles in 1911. The truck was the Swiss Saurer, shown above, during the first phase of its historic transcontinental journey.

Reo Archives

Sixty-four vehicles took part in the 1911 Glidden Tour, one of them being this four-cylinder Reo truck equipped with pneumatic tires. It carried baggage and equipment for other participants in the New York-to-Florida junket of 1,396 miles. Up to this point only solid rubber tires were considered practical for commercial vehicles.

commercial vehicles. The magazine further decided that something had to be done about the design of delivery wagons which seriously restricted the vision of the drivers. It decried the traditional body styles of horse-drawn vehicles as being totally unsafe for motor trucks. It said:

"A well-trained horse will often prevent a collision with an intersecting vehicle through its instinct of self-preservation, but with the motor vehicle there is no such safeguard, and all safety depends upon the alertness of the driver and his facilities for watching the road in all directions."

The horse, it seems, had had his day—but simple horse-sense was still being appreciated!

In April of 1904 New York City was the scene of a second commercial vehicle test, much more extensive than the first. There were 18 starters in the six-day competition; they included three Knoxes, two Olds, two Electric Vehicle Columbias, two Pope Waverleys, two Commercial Motor Company steam wagons, a Rockliff gasoline, a Union gasoline, a Consolidated gasoline, a Lansden electric, a Cantono electric fore carriage and a Fischer gas-electric combination.

The trade press hailed the contest as proof positive that the motor truck was ready to tackle transportation assignments ranging from tiny packages to five-ton loads. Prizes were won by the following trucks in various weight-carrying classifications:

Make	Weight, Pounds	Load, Pounds	Miles	Running Time	Deliveries
Olds	1,225	500	228¼	28.59	282
Columbia	2,455	1,100	184⅞	25.20	260
Cantono	2,000	1,700	145⅛	23.42	187
Consolidated	3,450	2,500	239½	25.39	150
Union	6,850	4,000	172⅞	29.30	109
Electric Vehicle	6,700	5,000	150¼	24.27	127
Fischer	14,050	10,000	187½	33.44	76

Automobile Manufacturers Association, Inc.

Between 1908 and 1910 William Crapo Durant bought out 25 rival manufacturers in the expansion of General Motors. One of them was the Randolph Motor Car Company which had a brief fling as a truck producer.

Jerrold B. Winther

This Winther quad-drive showed its capabilities on the Lake Michigan sand dunes for publicity purposes. The Winther Company operated from 1916 to 1922. It succumbed, not because of the failure of its trucks, but because surplus military vehicles knocked the bottom out of new sales.

Some historians believe that trucking, as a separate industry, had its beginning with the 1903 road test. Whether this is true or not is immaterial, but within the next three years there was a notable upsurge in truck manufacturing. In May of 1904 the Automobile Club of America staged the nation's first motor car parade in New York City. Of the 227 entries, 73 vehicles were classified as business wagons. That same month similar parades were also held in Boston and Chicago.

Meanwhile, the tour idea was becoming an important factor in the promotion of automotive travel. In 1903 the National Association of Automobile Manufacturers sponsored an endurance run from New York to Pittsburgh and drew 34 entries. The next year the American Automobile Association—which had been established in Chicago in 1902—sponsored a junket from New York to the Louisiana Purchase Exposition in St. Louis, 1,218 miles away. Eighteen cars started the trip which was marred by dissension, lost drivers, innumerable breakdowns and continual confrontations along the way with the local constabulary. This might have marked the end of organized touring had it not been for one of the participants.

Charles J. Glidden, a Boston industrialist who had already made a 50,000-mile round-the-world tour in an English Napier, enjoyed the St. Louis trip in spite of the bickering. He believed future

So-called "economy runs" were good promotion gimmicks as competition in the truck industry got tougher and tougher after World War I. Like many other automobile manufacturers, Maxwell also made some trucks.

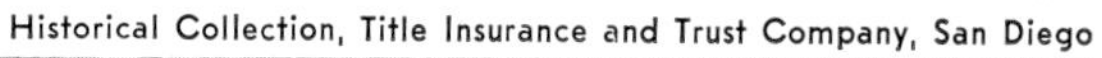

Historical Collection, Title Insurance and Trust Company, San Diego

Los Angeles County Museum of History

The American Locomotive Company built the Alco truck which was one of the 300-plus names which came and went before 1925. The vehicle shown here had just completed a transcontinental run from Philadelphia to San Francisco, with appropriate ceremonies, including a brass band and representatives from City Hall.

tours should be held, and he promptly drew up some rules to govern them. The first so-called Glidden Tour was an 870-mile round-trip journey from New York City to Bretton Woods, New Hampshire, and back. It was a seven-day event in which 33 automobiles participated. More than twice that many entries were on hand for the 1906 tour from Buffalo, New York, to Bretton Woods by way of Montreal and Quebec. The entry list that year included a Rapid Truck.

The Glidden Tours continued through 1913, focusing a spotlight on inter-city travel. While most of the participating vehicles were passenger cars, baggage-toting trucks were also involved, thus indicating the possibilities of extending their commercial use to deliveries between cities and to outlying rural customers. In 1911 R. E. Olds, who had participated himself as a driver six years earlier, introduced a new pneumatic-tired Reo truck to the Glidden Tour. It was an early step in the ultimate transition away from solid rubber.

A sure sign that trucks were coming of age was the publication in 1906 of *Power Wagon* and *The Commercial Vehicle,* trade periodicals devoted exclusively to the truck industry. At the same time, the major auto shows in New York's Madison Square Garden and the First Regiment Armory in Chicago established separate divisions for business machines.

Among the entries grouped together in the basement of Madison Square Garden that year were a three-ton Packard with reinforced wood frame, three air-cooled Knoxes, five Studebaker electrics, six Vehicle Equipment Company electrics ranging from 1,000 pounds to five tons, two Hewitt gasoline chain drives, four Electric Vehicle Columbias, a 12-horsepower Franklin, a one-ton Olds wagon, a two-ton Pope driven by a gasoline engine placed crosswise under the seat and several Pope Waverley electrics.

More and more new makes were appearing on the scene, each with an innovation or two to separate them from others in their class. With

Jerrold B. Winther

(Above) The Jeffery four-wheel-drive truck ultimately became the well-known Nash Quad of World War I. Thomas B. Jeffery, a long-time bicycle manufacturer, had become famous for his line of Rambler automobiles produced in Kenosha, Wisconsin. He died in 1910, and his son—Charles T., a survivor of the Lusitania sinking—continued the company until it was sold to Nash in 1916. (Below) A favorite method of demonstrating FWDs was to drive them up courthouse steps. This particular exhibition took place in Memphis, Tennessee.

FWD Corporation

limited advertising outlets, manufacturers depended upon public demonstrations and exhibitions to promote their vehicles. It became evident to them, though, that the organized contest was not always the best medium. Races and endurance runs were fine—if you won—but if your truck went mechanically awry or limped home a dismal last, the publicity value of such a showing was anything but good.

So gradually individual truck-makers turned to staging their own "contests," against time and distance rather than competitive vehicles. They took the form of speed dashes between cities, inter-state runs or more ambitious transcontinental excursions. Then, only the successful ones were publicized.

The first cross-country journey by a truck was accomplished in 1911 by a Swiss Saurer—but it was a disjointed two-stage project. The trip started in Denver on March 4 and took 66 laborious days to cross the mountains and cover the 1,500 miles to Los Angeles. Then the seven-ton freighter lumbered northward to San Francisco where it was loaded on a railroad car and shipped to Pueblo, Colorado. From there it started the eastward leg of its journey to New York City on June 12.

It was a milestone for the trucking industry which was not surpassed until the following year when a Packard truck carried a three-ton load from New York to San Francisco in just 46 days. That same year—1912—500 trucks participated in a commercial wagon parade in Philadelphia.

There were many other tests of strength, of endurance, of economy, of new equipment and other automotive selling points. The promotion technique inevitably culminated in a publicity man's dream, when Miss Luella Bates—"a mere slip of a girl"—piloted a three-ton Four Wheel Drive on a transcontinental trip, after first driving the vehicle from the FWD plant in Clintonville, Wisconsin, to the New York Auto Show of 1920. She was one of six female drivers selected by the company to demonstrate the steering ease and maneuverability of the big trucks which played such a vital role during World War I.

In a few short years scores of trucks came and went, some of them because of financial difficul-

FWD Corporation

(Above) The FWD Corporation accomplished a publicity coup in 1919-20 when it used a pretty and petite woman pilot to demonstrate the maneuverability and driving-ease of its vehicles. Miss Luella Bates, shown here, first took a Four Wheel Drive to the New York Auto Show and followed that with a transcontinental jaunt. Five other lady drivers were selected from plant workers to demonstrate company trucks. (Below) Cross-country trips were scheduled by truck promoters in the scramble to prove the capabilities of motor vehicles for inter-state hauling.

Automobile Manufacturers Association, Inc.

Harrah's Automobile Collection, Reno, Nevada

A running time of 32 hours, 40½ minutes was the record set by this 3½-ton Fageol on an 878-mile speed run between San Francisco and Los Angeles and return. Sewell Cushion Wheels and Goodrich De Luxe Tires were given much credit for the 26.8 mph average speed which topped the best performance by a pneumatic-tired truck.

ties and other business vagaries; others simply didn't measure up to the demands of the ultimate users. But along the way, each new make contributed something to the final product—even if it merely proved that one principle or another wouldn't work.

The Waterless Knox, so successful in history's first organized competition, faded and disappeared. The early coal-burning steamers proved impractical because of the logistics of fuel supply. The chain-drive principle, so important during the initial decades of trucking, suddenly became obsolete.

As the experimentation and testing went on, better and better trucks evolved. All of the award-winners of the 1903-1904 contests were lost in the shuffle. So, too, was the first transcontinental Saurer. The giant shakedown period from the mid-1890s through 1915 took a huge toll of hopeful manufacturers. Those who survived faced an even more rigorous testing ground—on the battlefields of World War I.

The Goodyear Tire & Rubber Company

Immediately after World War I this Goodyear truck set a new speed record for coast-to-coast travel by commercial vehicles, going from Los Angeles to New York in 13 days and five hours. For a brief time Goodyear used its own experimental trucks and buses in such demonstrations to prove the worth of its pneumatic tires.

Seattle Chamber of Commerce

A ton of Carnation condensed milk was delivered in New York City on September 19, 1916, by this GMC truck after a transcontinental run from Seattle beginning on July 12. The truck was driven by William Warwick, who was accompanied by his wife. The Seattle Chamber of Commerce sponsored the historic junket.

Transcontinental Milk Run:

From Seattle to New York in 31 Gruelling Days

ONE OF THE MOST UNUSUAL and most ambitious of the pioneer test tours was a 1916 transcontinental junket from Seattle, Washington, to New York City.

It was sponsored by the Seattle Chamber of Commerce, and had, as its prime mission, the goal of promoting the so-called National Parks Highway.

An intrepid truck jockey—William Warwick—and his equally courageous wife agreed to make the lengthy trip. To show their confidence in the venture, they also decided to take their infant daughter with them.

A 1½-ton GMC stock truck, straight out of a factory shipment, was selected as the vehicle to tackle the arduous assignment. The Carnation Company loaded the truck with a ton of evaporated milk which Warwick was to carry to prove that the road from Seattle to New York would accommodate the heaviest known passenger automobile—with a ton to spare.

On July 12 the GMC pulled out of the Puget Sound city on its mid-summer sojourn. Then, with the cheers of the well-wishers behind him, Driver Warwick began to consider the conditions under which he had accepted the ignition keys.

Absolutely no outside help would be permitted to get him out of any trouble. The truck carried only the standard equipment and tool kit, and the rules stated that no chains, ropes, planks or similar gear could be included in the load. A tow or shove from another vehicle was absolutely verboten.

At Blewett's Pass across the Cascade Mountains—less than 100 miles from Seattle—gamblers were wagering 25 to 1 that the truck would never get beyond that point. The Warwicks wondered for a while if the bettors weren't right, especially when they watched a Metz roadster miss a turn and go hurtling down into a 1,500-foot chasm.

But the GMC slogged ahead, bringing them out of the mountains into the mud of the Columbia River valley. Somehow the Warwicks dug their truck out of one axle-deep predicament after another as they struggled across central Washington on the way to Spokane.

For 14 hours a day the hardy travelers stayed on the road, across northern Idaho, through Butte to Miles City, Montana. In North Dakota an unexpected complication occurred, as the Warwick youngster became ill and arrangements had to be made to have her sent home. Still, the touring couple persisted, and as roads got better in the flatlands of the Middle West, their daily mileage improved considerably.

Their itinerary took them to Minneapolis, to Chicago, Cleveland, Buffalo, Albany and finally—on September 19—to Gotham itself. The truck's recordograph registered 3,710 miles when the load of milk was delivered to the New York consignee. Thirty-one days of actual driving time were involved, but exactly ten weeks separated the start from the finish. If the truth were known, Warwick probably spent more time with his hands on a shovel than on the steering wheel. Altogether, the trip log showed that the GMC had broken through 43 bridges and culverts in the course of the cross-country jaunt. This was hardly an indication that the National Parks Highway was ready for a flood of tourist traffic!

Wherever a rotten bridge gave way, however, the local citizenry moved to repair and improve the crossing. As the result of the publicity created by the trip, many stretches of the road received renewed attention, and the Warwicks left a better highway behind them than the one they had crossed.

Undaunted by their rigorous experiences, the automotive voyageurs headed homeward by a southerly route. They drove on long stretches of the Lincoln Memorial Highway which a year earlier had been well traveled by motorists going

Driver William Warwick worked diligently to extricate his mud-bound GMC on the last lap of his 9,513-mile journey. His self-imposed rules required that he accept no help in conditions like this to prove that a driver could manage a transcontinental trip without the aid of mules, horses or other trucks.

Seattle Post-Intelligencer Library

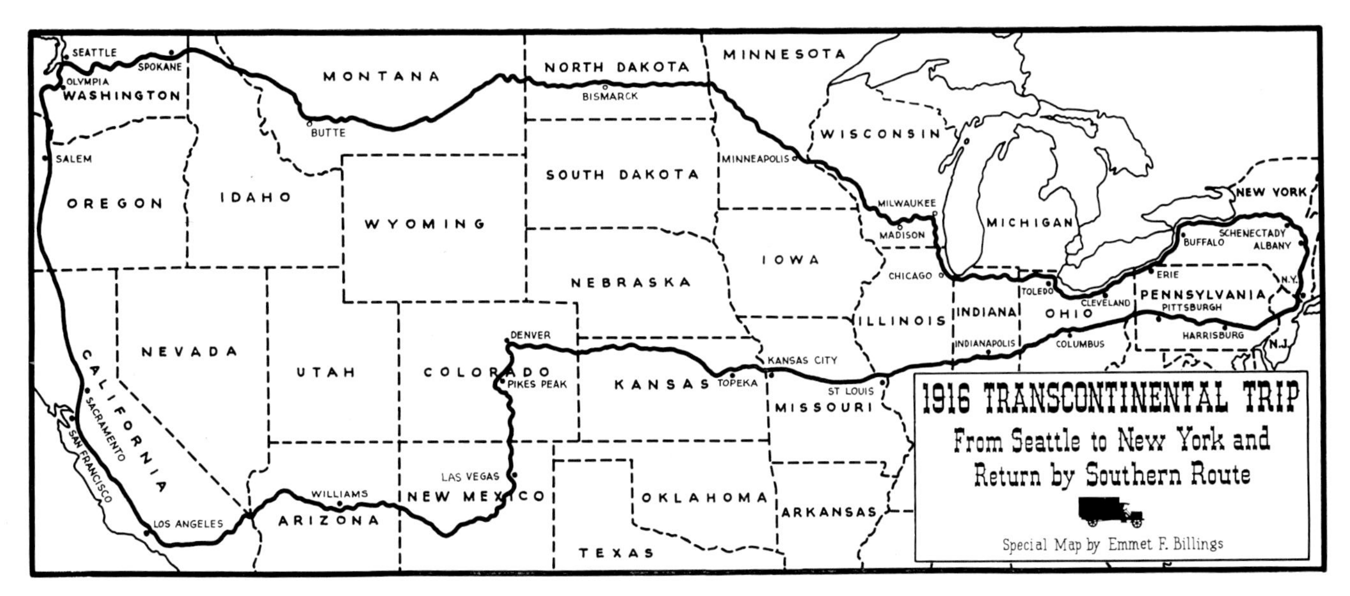

The Seattle-to-New York junket had as one of its missions the promotion of the so-called National Parks Highway. The Seattle Chamber of Commerce wanted to prove that motorists from the East could make it over America's most scenic route. Driver Warwick selected a southerly itinerary for the return trip.

to the Panama-Pacific Exposition in San Francisco. From Denver, the Warwicks turned southward to Santa Fe and Los Angeles before making the long coastal run back to Seattle.

All in all, they traveled 9,513 miles through 24 states under anything but ideal conditions. The banners on their truck delivered a strong message on behalf of motor travel, and the news release they distributed in every city and hamlet in which they stopped on their return trip appealed for more and better roads. It said:

"The great transcontinental highways of this country are going to become important factors in our national lives. In a sense they are more valuable than railroads, for the transcontinental railway trains make few stops and carry only a limited number of passengers, but there is no limit to the number of motor vehicles which can go back and forth along a great highway . . . which enriches every city and town along its route. Your town is situated along such a national highway.

"But there is something else to think about. There is no greater defense in time of war than a great transcontinental highway. A navy may be sunk, the Panama Canal may be blocked up, a railroad is only a thin band of metal . . . a section of track may be torn up and interrupt the railroad for several days. But a great highway cannot be destroyed."

To say the least, the Warwick odyssey was an outstanding success. It marked another milestone in the still brief history of trucking.

Seattle Chamber of Commerce

The Warwicks' truck was a standard 1½-ton GMC just as it came from the factory. The Seattle Chamber of Commerce, which sponsored the gruelling trip, had the vehicle properly emblazoned with appropriate publicity signs. A ton of Carnation evaporated milk — a Washington State product — was the selected cargo. Goodrich solid rubber tires were used on the truck, a fact which the manufacturer proudly advertised, especially after the tires held up all the way to New York and on part of the return trip.

(Opposite page) FWD Corporation

FWD Corporation

Troopers of General Pershing's command on the Mexican border practiced a little "dry run" shooting aboard an FWD Model B converted to a tank truck. In the pursuit of Pancho Villa, the U. S. Army used trucks and automobiles on a full scale for the first time. As it turned out, the experience was soon to be valuable in World War I.

America's Trucks Go to War

CAPTAIN ALEXANDER E. WILLIAMS, a tall West Pointer from North Carolina, had nothing personal against horses and mules, but while other army officers in 1911 saw little need to disturb the transportation status quo, Williams emerged as a prime exponent of the motor truck for military purposes.

With his pen and personal persuasiveness, he propounded the thesis that animal power had become obsolete and that a modern army ultimately must turn to self-propelled vehicles. Though he spelled out his ideas in the *Infantry Journal,* there was anything but a breathless rush to adopt his concept. Fortunately, he had had a four-year assignment with the Quartermaster Corps, time enough for him to develop a campaign to prove, once and for all, that trucks could do a more efficient job in the field than time-tested horses and mules.

(Opposite page) The famed Four Wheel Drive "Scout Car" which participated in the first major test of motor vehicles by the U. S. Army. In the mud-spattered truck were Frank Dorn, driver; Capt. A. E. Williams, officer in charge of the test, and Jimmy Gaughan, mechanic.

His theories didn't *exactly* fall on deaf ears. After all, the U. S. Army already owned 12 of the estimated 25,000 trucks in the country. Three were assigned to the Quartermaster Depot in San Francisco; one was located at Fort Sam Houston, Texas; another was at the Military Academy at West Point; and the remaining seven had been shipped overseas to Manila.

But even before the turn of the century, there was some official interest in motorized military vehicles. In 1895 Major General Nelson A. Miles, an elderly veteran of the Civil War and the Indian campaigns which followed, succeeded to the command of the army. In spite of his age and past service, he was an imaginative officer who recognized that technical changes were on the horizon. He was responsible for an experimental bicycle troop in 1897, and a year earlier his official report called for the introduction of motor wagons into army service. But even as commandant, he was unable to overcome custom and tradition, and he fretted continually about the

Brigadier General Alexander E. Williams, as a foresighted captain in 1912, played a major role in the development of the trucking industry when he persuaded his superiors in the U. S. Army to give motor vehicles a thorough test, to see if they could stand the rigors demanded by military transportation.

progress made by European armies in the use of trucks, while his own command lagged behind.

When he retired in 1903, he wrote a long letter to the Secretary of War, recommending that five motorized regiments be organized to replace a similar number of cavalry units. He prophesied that self-propelled transportation "will be utilized in the next war" and he further recommended the improvement of roads throughout the nation. His cavalry compatriots were indignant, and his suggestions—like so many others—were filed.

In 1902 the Ordnance Department bought a forge and battery wagon from the U. S. Long Distance Automobile Company, and the following year, the Surgeon General asked the White Sewing Machine Company of Cleveland to work on an experimental ambulance. But peace-time armies have always been notorious for approaching innovations of any kind at snail's pace, and that was the problem which faced Captain Williams in his eagerness to vindicate his beliefs.

Unlike Billy Mitchell and his celebrated effort to create an air force, Williams did not have to do battle with superiors whose minds were totally closed to change. True, he faced lethargy and skepticism, but General James B. Aleshire, the Quartermaster General, gave the young motor-minded officer enough leeway to pursue a course of action.

The first step was to draw up specifications for a standardized army truck; at the same time two motor vehicles were purchased for experimental purposes. One was a 1¼-ton chain-drive model built by the Alden Sampson Manufacturing Company of Detroit, and the other was a 1½-ton shaft-drive White. Captain Williams was detailed by the War Department to visit truck manufacturers to discuss army requirements with them and the possibilities of a practical test under military convoy conditions.

His trek took him to the Sampson and Ford factories in Detroit; to the Garford plant in Elyria, Ohio; to the White Company in Cleveland and to Mack headquarters in Allentown, Pennsylvania. Words like "impractical" and "impossible" greeted his presentation for a standard military truck, and when the manufacturers heard the requirements for cross-country use of their vehicles, they were less than enthusiastic. They were confident of their trucks' capabilities on good roads, but they were not so sure of performance off the beaten path.

Captain Williams was understandably disappointed. He had not counted upon negativism from the men who might stand to gain the most. It was at this point, in late 1911, that he came upon a small advertisement extolling a new vehicle which the builders—in the unlikely town of Clintonville, Wisconsin—claimed could operate in sand or mud because power was applied to all four wheels. Williams took the ad to General Aleshire,

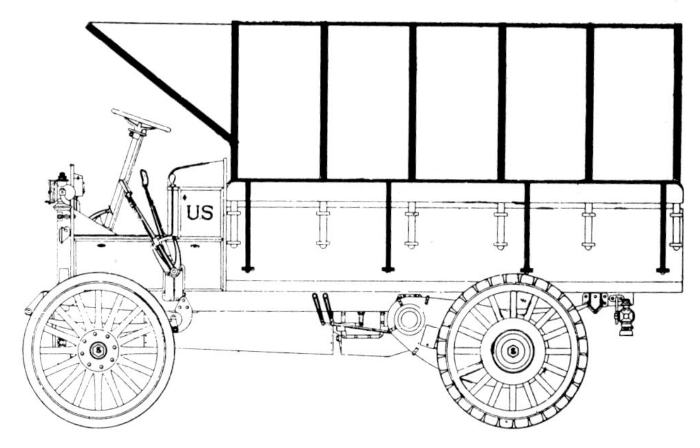

Fourth truck in the 1912 test was a chain-drive Sampson. On the second day out of Washington, D. C., it broke through the ice fording a creek, then burned out its connecting rod bearings trying to climb a slippery hill. It was withdrawn from the tour and shipped back to Washington, D. C.

U. S. Signal Corps Photo in The National Archives

Thanks to the persistence of Captain Williams and others like him, the Army was at least aware of the potential of trucks before World War I. In the post-war era, further tests were conducted, including the first transcontinental convoy in 1919. On the latter trek, this truck was stuck near North Platte, Nebraska.

who agreed that the principle was worth investigating and who promptly authorized another trip for the captain—to the plant of the Four Wheel Drive Auto Company in Wisconsin.

The first impression was anything but convincing. Otto Zachow and William Besserdich, blacksmith-machinists who had designed and built the new auto, were trying to finish five cars in the cramped confines of their tiny shop. Their first vehicle—called the "Battleship"—had been delivered, but a second was on hand to give Captain Williams a thorough introduction to four-wheel-drive efficiency.

The company driver—24-year-old Frank Dorn —gave the visiting officer the complete repertory. He drove the touring car (the firm had not yet built a truck) through mudholes, across plowed fields, in and out of sand pits and even up the steps of the local Lutheran church. Captain Williams was amazed and so reported to General Aleshire. Walter A. Olen, president of the embryonic company, offered to release a car to the army for further testing, but the Quartermaster General decided to buy one—for $1,940—and to have it shipped to Fort Myer, Virginia, to be fitted with an army escort wagon box.

Meanwhile, plans for an extended road test were being developed. Captain Williams, whose tour with the Quartermaster Corps had ended, was assigned to the 19th Infantry and then ordered back to the Q.M.G.O. for the duration of

FWD Corporation

Stripped down, the FWD "Scout Car" looked like this. With a truck body added, it was one of three vehicles to complete the gruelling 1,504-mile run from Washington, D. C., to Fort Benjamin Harrison in 1912.

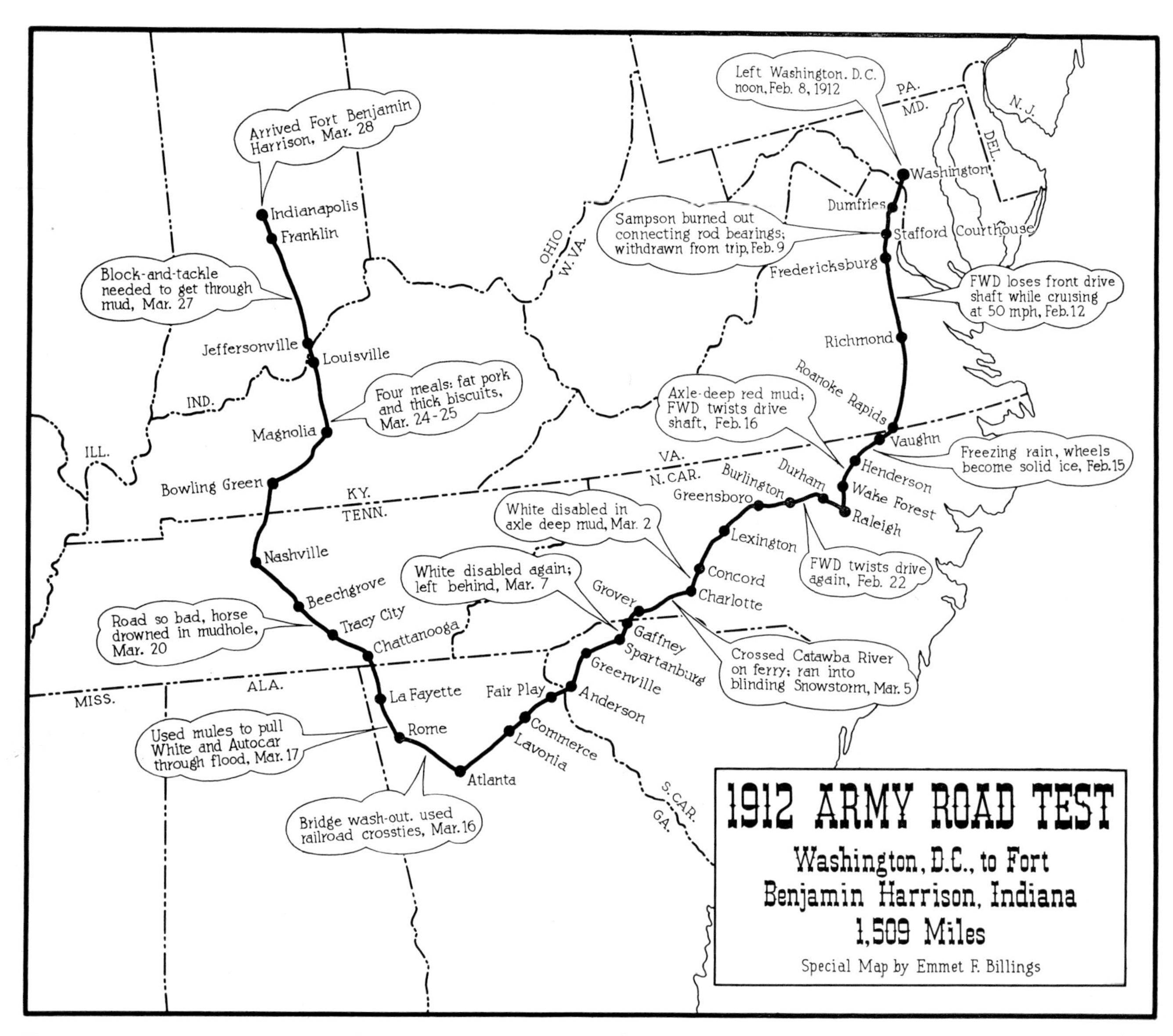

This map, prepared by Emmet F. Billings, traces the route of the 1912 U. S. Army road test, planned to determine whether or not trucks could replace horses and mules under field conditions. Three vehicles—a White, an Autocar and an FWD—successfully completed the trip to set the stage for a giant revolution in military logistics.

the truck experiment. When the itinerary for the trial was revealed, it sounded as if it had been planned by the horse-and-mule faction to thwart the encroachments of the motor truck. Loaded with supplies, plus a ton and a half of sand ballast, the vehicles were expected to travel more than 1,500 miles over the most primitive of roads —and in winter weather. The route (see map above) was to take them from Washington, D. C., via Atlanta, Georgia, to Fort Benjamin Harrison near Indianapolis. The date of departure was set for February 8, 1912.

Organizing the convoy had its complications. The Four Wheel Drive with its new truck box was ready to go. So was the army-owned Sampson. Only White and Autocar had accepted the government invitation to participate independently, and each entered a 1½-ton stock truck. A Wilcox Truck Company entry, as well as the White truck which the army had bought the previous year, were withdrawn just before the tour started. At noon, on the appointed day, the quartet of pioneer motor trucks lumbered out of the nation's capital. General Aleshire probably unnerved Captain Williams with his parting remark:

". . . when your trucks get stuck, just wire me and I'll send you some mules!"

The following edited version of Captain Williams' trip log describes the unusual and difficult journey which marked a milestone in early trucking history:

1,509 Miles of Mud, Muck and Miseries

February 8: Left Washington, D. C., noon. Autocar sheared off bolts on driving shaft. Sampson unable to climb snow-covered hill; had to pull her up with block-and-tackle. Arrived Dumfries, Va., 33 miles.

February 9: Sampson broke through ice into a ditch. Autocar rejoined convoy. More trouble for Sampson on ice-covered hill; burned out connecting rod bearings. Sampson left behind. Arrived Stafford Courthouse, Va., 16 miles.

February 10: Sampson shipped back to Washington. Arrived Fredericksburg, Va., 10 miles.

February 11: Sunday, stayed in Fredericksburg.

February 12: Forward drive shaft dropped out on road as FWD was cruising at 50 mph. Repaired immediately. Arrived Richmond, Va., 60 miles.

February 13: Good roads. Arrived Roanoke Rapids, N. C., 98 miles (longest one-day run of complete convoy).

February 14: Steering gear of FWD broken. Finally arrived Vaughn, N. C.

February 15: Light rain which froze as it fell. Truck wheels became solid cakes of ice. Ran in low gear continuously. Arrived Henderson, N. C., 30 miles.

February 16: Red mud axle deep. Had to leave road and travel cross-country trail. Built bridge to cross stream. FWD twisted off drive shaft. Picked up a young girl and escort and took them to dance in Wake Forest, N. C., 30 miles.

February 17: Towed FWD to Wake Forest, left it for repairs. Arrived Raleigh, N. C., 25 miles.

February 18: Sunday, stayed in Raleigh.

February 19: Picked up new transmission for FWD, returned to Wake Forest to repair it. Back to Raleigh.

February 20: Roads mostly macadam. Arrived Durham, N. C., 25 miles.

February 21: Heavy rain. Advanced yard at a time on Morgan Hill through deep mud. Stopped for night at farmhouse, 20 miles.

February 22: FWD twisted drive shaft again. Left behind. Arrived Burlington, N. C., 25 miles.

February 23: So muddy even got stuck on down-grades. Arrived Greensboro, N. C., 23 miles, to await arrival of new drive shaft for FWD.

February 23-26: Remained in Greensboro.

February 27: Drive shaft arrived. Returned to FWD.

February 28: Repairs completed about noon. Returned to Greensboro.

February 29: Ran into stiff red mud. Required three hours to make final three miles. Arrived Lexington, N. C., 36 miles.

March 1: Accident to FWD, three hours to repair. Arrived Concord, N. C., 40 miles.

March 2: While traveling through axle-deep mud, White disabled. Left behind. Arrived Charlotte, N. C., 23 miles. Telegraphed New York for White parts.

March 3: Parts delivered, amazing speed.

March 4: White repaired and brought to Charlotte.

March 5: Crossed Catawba River on rickety ferry. Truck broke mooring chain and set boat adrift. Arrived Grover, N. C., in blinding snowstorm, 45 miles.

March 6: White mired in mud, three hours to free. Farmers brought hot coffee and biscuits. Arrived Gaffney, S. C., 16 miles.

March 7: White disabled again. Arrived Cowpens, S. C., 16 miles.

March 8: Left White and two mechanics. FWD to Anderson, S. C., 80 miles; Autocar to Greenville, 45 miles.

March 9: FWD to Commerce, Ga., 70 miles; Autocar to Fair Play, 56 miles.

March 10: FWD to Atlanta, Ga., 80 miles; Autocar reached Ashland. Parts arrived in Cowpens.

March 11: White repaired, reached Lavonia, Ga., 112 miles. Autocar arrived in Atlanta.

March 12-15: Awaiting White; arrived in Atlanta on 15th.

March 16: Bridge washout. Crossed stream on railroad crossties. Arrived Rome, Ga., 69 miles.

March 17: Twice crossed flooded areas. Hired mules to pull White and Autocar through. FWD's carburetor mounted high enough to permit it to drive through. Arrived La Fayette, 45 miles.

March 18: Arrived Chattanooga, Tenn., 30 miles.

March 19: Had to arrange for government launch to tow ferry boat with trucks across Tennessee River. Arrived Tracy City, Tenn., 46 miles.

March 20: Road so bad a horse drowned in mudhole before it could be unhitched. Arrived Beechgrove, Tenn., 45 miles.

March 21: Good roads. Arrived Nashville, Tenn., 50 miles.

March 22: Arrived Bowling Green, Ky., 57 miles.

March 23: Arrived Magnolia, Ky., 75 miles over very good roads.

March 24: Sunday, remained in Magnolia. Ate fat pork and thick biscuits Saturday night and three times Sunday.

March 25: Fat pork and biscuits for breakfast. Arrived Louisville, Ky.

March 26: Picked up supplies at Jeffersonville, Ind., for Fort Benjamin Harrison. Hit bad mud late in afternoon. Forced to sleep in schoolhouse.

March 27: Used telephone poles and block-and-tackle to get trucks through mud. Arrived Franklin, Ind., 75 miles.

March 28: Reached Fort Benjamin Harrison. Total distance: 1,509 miles.

FWD Corporation

Following the major test tour from Washington, D. C., to Fort Benjamin Harrison, the army decided to sponsor a second field trial, also in 1912. Six different makes of trucks were assigned as supply vehicles for a provisional regiment on a march from Dubuque, Iowa, to Sparta, Wisconsin. Conditions were unusually bad as indicated by this photo showing an FWD fording a small stream.

Upon their arrival at Fort Benjamin Harrison, the three trucks were given a thorough inspection, which showed no appreciable wear or damage to the engines. Captain Williams had kept a careful record of the entire trip to help in future design and specifications for military vehicles. His log showed that the White truck averaged a little more than 5½ miles to a gallon of gasoline and 127 miles to a gallon of oil. The FWD averaged a fraction over 4 miles to a gallon of gas and 109 miles to a gallon of oil. The Autocar used a gallon of fuel every 4½ miles and a gallon of oil every 60 miles.

Unfortunately, the road test was not recognized as an important success by the military hierarchy, and there was no immediate stampede to convert army transportation to motorized units. Captain Williams had estimated that the trip would be completed in approximately three weeks, and it took more than twice that time. "Army grey beards," as *Automobile Topics* called the military truck-knockers, pointed to the mechanical problems and the mud miseries as clear indications that four-wheeled self-powered vehicles would never measure up to their favored four-footed beasts of burden.

But Captain Williams and the truck manufacturers had scored a point, even though the results were not immediate. They proved that trucks—at least three different makes—had been developed to a point where they could be depended upon in the back-country and that ultimately their day would come. Meanwhile, the army decided to try one more test before it sent Captain Williams back to the 19th Infantry at Fort Meade, South Dakota.

The plan was to use motor trucks to supply a provisional regiment during a practice march from Dubuque, Iowa, to Sparta, Wisconsin. By this time the army had repaired both its original White and the Sampson which had fared so badly on the first trial. Both were shipped to Fort Benjamin Harrison where the government FWD was also in readiness. Captain Williams was ordered to take the three vehicles to Dubuque where three other 1½-ton trucks — a Kelly-

U. S. trucks "went to war" for the first time in 1916 when General John J. Pershing led a punitive expedition against Pancho Villa and his bandits. This painting depicts a train of White trucks crossing the Chihuahua desert. Of the 74 "trains" of motor vehicles involved in the campaign, 20 of them were Whites.

White Motor Corporation

White Motor Corporation

The Mexican campaign in 1916 was a prelude to World War I and an unusual testing ground for motor vehicles being used in combat for the first time by the U. S. Army. The problems of supply, performance and repair were many, with one of the major weaknesses being a lack of experienced drivers. (Top) Despite the handicaps, hundreds of supply sorties were successfully completed by trains of trucks like the Whites shown here. (Center) A convoy of Whites leaving Columbus, New Mexico, with supplies for the field base at Colonia Dublan, Mexico. (Bottom) Another unit of Whites heading out into the waterless, roadless desert, typical of the Mexican campaign.

FWD Corporation

An attack by Pancho Villa on the tiny town of Columbus, New Mexico, on March 8-9, 1916, resulted in the punitive expedition ordered by President Woodrow Wilson. Columbus became a supply point for the U. S. Army forces and was the scene of one of the first military motor pools. Some 4,000 motor vehicles were ultimately involved.

Springfield, a Mack and a Kato—were rented. In addition, six 3-ton models—a White, a Packard, a Saurer, a Velie, a Graham and a Four Wheel Drive—were also leased for the trial. The latter were to be used to replace the railroads in re-supplying the field trains out of the two main supply bases at Dubuque and Madison, Wisconsin. Cost of the rented trucks was listed as $12.00 a day, including driver and repairs.

White Motor Corporation

Captain Williams had invited representatives of truck companies to witness the march which got underway in early June; he wanted them to see first-hand the demands on a military vehicle so that they might be better prepared to overcome any design deficiencies. Some of the problems, as it turned out, would have to be solved by the army, too. In the beginning, the trucks were greatly overloaded, which hampered their efficiency. The lighter models, which were assigned to companies in place of their regular mule-drawn field wagons, were forced to operate at the speed of the foot soldier which caused considerable overheating of motors. Worst of all, though, the old mud bugaboo was ever present to complicate matters.

Again, this test was not a roaring success, but for Captain Williams and a small coterie of truck supporters, this was another step forward. Interestingly enough, Williams' report praised the White, Mack (though it needed more power) and FWD trucks, those which were to survive through years of development and competition.

(Top) Troops and vehicles of Truck Company No. 45 at Fort Bliss, Texas, during the Mexican border disturbance. (Center) Loaded with rations and fuel, these White trucks were about to depart in search of a missing aviator. (Bottom) A fleet of White trucks of the Third U. S. Aero Squadron at Fort Sam Houston, Texas.

Of the others he wrote:

"The Kelly 1½-ton truck was withdrawn the second day out because of engine trouble. . . . The Sampson was no good at all except on smooth hard roads. The Kato, although four-wheel-drive, did not prove satisfactory, due to the fact the power was not properly applied."

The inevitable process of the survival of the fittest had come to the truck industry!

The departure of Captain Williams was a noticeable blow to the cause of motorized military transportation, but the seed had been planted, and the slow process of transition was underway. How long this would have taken under normal peacetime conditions will never be known, because history added a massive catalyst.

In 1914 World War I exploded over Europe, and just as General Miles had predicted, motorized transport became a vital factor right from the start. When General Gallieni's famed "taxicab army" saved Paris in the first Battle of the Marne, it should have been obvious that a new era had dawned—and still U. S. military planners dawdled. Meanwhile, American automobile and truck manufacturers were forced into high gear to fill military orders for European armies.

White Motor Corporation

The Mexican campaign offered every imaginable type of obstacle to the use of trucks: heat, dust, 7,000-foot altitudes, drifting sand, intense cold in the mountains, boulder-strewn trails—and the inevitable mud!

Another two years went by, and then a Mexican bandit named Doroteo Arango (more popularly known as Pancho Villa), created the incident which was to accomplish what General Miles, Captain Williams and other truck enthusiasts were unable to do. Following Villa's attack on Columbus, New Mexico, on March 8-9, 1916, President Woodrow Wilson sent an expedition led by

Thousands of American-made trucks were shipped to the A.E.F. in France, but right up until the Armistice, General Pershing was demanding thousands more. The motor vehicles had proved their worth in the logistics of war.

U. S. Signal Corps Photo in The National Archives

FWD Corporation

A World War I ordnance truck convoy rested before resuming its supply mission. In full camouflage dress, these FWDs from Clintonville, Wisconsin, became a common sight on the battle-scarred roads of France.

Brigadier General John J. Pershing to capture the outlaw. Though the famed general never did catch Villa, the campaign had a military by-product which had not been anticipated.

When Pershing arrived in Mexico, the U. S. Army had less than 1,000 motor vehicles of all types scattered about its far-flung commands. So when the general called for five motorized trains — 27 trucks to the train — consternation reigned at the War Department and among manufacturers who were already burdened by war orders. And that was just the beginning. Before the campaign ended, army reports indicated that 70 such trains were in action as American forces penetrated 400 miles into the Mexican interior. In his own memoirs, Pershing wrote that his organization included 22 companies of 25 trucks each, with complete repair shops and a large depot of spare parts at Columbus.

The failure to prepare was obvious. Without standardized equipment, the results were inevitable. Before the 11-month campaign was over, 128 different makes and models of motor vehicles were in use on the border. Among the trucks were Jefferys, Whites, Packards, Locomobile-Rikers, FWDs, Pierce-Arrows, Fords and many

(Opposite page) Top: Doughboy mechanics assembling GMC trucks at Saint Nazaire, France. Bottom: At the great supply base of Saint Nazaire, a single quad-drive truck pulled ten loaded trailers.

U. S. Signal Corps Photo in The National Archives

Trucks and horse-drawn vehicles shared the war-torn roads of the battle zone. Traffic conditions were unbelievable (the scene here was at Esnes, France, in September of 1918), but motor vehicles still managed to operate with enough effectiveness to keep front-line units supplied and at fighting strength.

Automobile Manufacturers Association, Inc.

others. Needless to say, the supply of spare parts was a fantastic mess. Secondly, the army didn't have the drivers and mechanics to operate and repair the vehicles, so civilians were hired initially to get the job done while the War Department scrambled to recruit qualified soldiers.

As bad as it was, Pershing managed to establish a semblance of order out of the chaos. Early attempts were made at developing armored cars. A bombastic young lieutenant named George Smith Patton, Jr., used three Dodge touring cars to roust a nest of bandits out of an adobe fortress at San Miguelito. Patton called his vehicles "modern warhorses." When Pershing and his so-called Punitive Expedition were recalled on February 15, 1917, an altogether different approach to military transport was being written into the manuals. As a prelude to World War I, the Mexican campaign had provided an unusually propitious training ground for American troops, and it had—at long last—proved the value of the motor vehicle to army logistics.

(Opposite page) Top: The children of Menancourt greeted these U. S. Marines aboard their battle-weary Packard. (Bottom) Motorized warfare was still in its infancy when this unit of doughboys rode into action "somewhere in France."

(Top) U. S. Signal Corps Photo in The National Archives; (Bottom) U. S. War Department General Staff Photo in The National Archives

While bigger trucks were playing an important role in troop movement and supply, the motorized ambulance—literally and figuratively—got its "baptism of fire" during World War I. There was little standardization, as many of the ambulances were donated by clubs and even private citizens. New York Elks provided the slim-tired models above. The people of Kansas City donated the trio of Whites directly below, while the State of Rhode Island sent the lone White (bottom) to the French in Paris.

White Motor Corporation

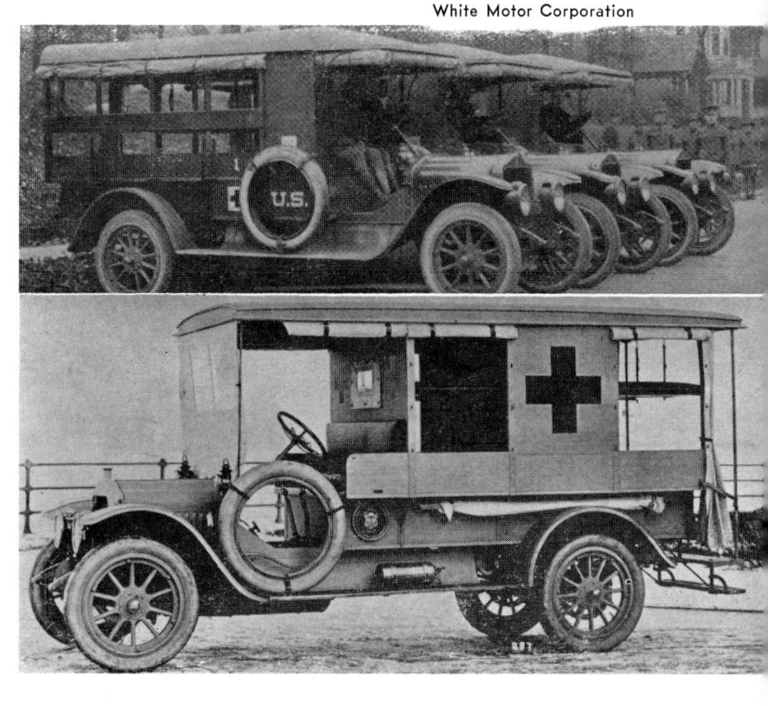

U. S. Signal Corps Photo in The National Archives

The roads of France were torn to shreds, not so much by shell-fire as by the endless traffic of supply trains and troop carriers. This picture was taken near Sansey in September of 1918.

The Women's Overseas Hospitals received the White ambulance (below) from the Sorosis organization of New York. (Bottom) World War I proved the need for specialty vehicles, so—among others—searchlight units were developed.

(Top) White Motor Corporation (Bottom) FWD Corporation

When Congress declared war on April 6, 1917, the U. S. Army had some 2,400 serviceable trucks, thanks indirectly to Pancho Villa. The same army had less than 1,500 machine guns of three different types and 55 airplanes, 51 of which were judged obsolete and the other four virtual junk heaps.

Again—in a new role—it would be "Black Jack" Pershing who would be calling for trucks and motor vehicles for his Expeditionary Force in France. When the first units of the A.E.F. sailed for Europe in June of 1917, several truck companies, composed of 70 men and 33 trucks each, were included in the contingent. But they were the proverbial drop-in-the-bucket as the demands of a major war were to prove. Following his arrival in France, Pershing estimated that ultimately he would need at least 50,000 motor vehicles and an unlimited reserve of spare parts. It is now history that he had to plead continually, not only for trucks, but for a thousand other military necessities.

He later wrote: "With our country by far the greatest producer in the world of automobiles and trucks, it was surprising that we were so poorly equipped with them . . . despite my most urgent appeals and the resulting promises from Washington, we had to borrow . . . large numbers of trucks from the French."

Even after the A.E.F. had ben in France for

more than a year, the problem continued. Pershing had established a Motor Transport Corps to consolidate that phase of his command. The M.T.C. proved effective, but the great bottleneck at home persisted.

"At that moment (the summer of 1918), when we were asking the French to lend us trucks, they made the same request of us," Pershing wrote. "We actually needed 1,300 automobiles, thousands of trucks and all other kinds of motor vehicles. The ambulance situation was critical; several sanitary units were completely immobile and twenty base hospitals had arrived without equipment."

That September, during the Meuse-Argonne drive, Pershing once again cabled the Chief of Staff in Washington, D. C.:

"At the present time our ability to supply and maneuver our forces depends largely on motor transportation. The shortage in motor transportation is particularly embarrassing now due to shortage of horses for our horse-drawn transport. We are able to carry out present plans due to fact that we have been able to borrow temporarily large numbers of trucks and ambulances from France. We have also borrowed fifteen American Ambulance sections from Italy. The shortage of ambulances to move our wounded is critical. . . . The need for motor transportation is urgent. It is not understood why greater advantage has not been taken of deck space to ship motor trucks. Trucks do not overburden dock accommodations or require railroad transportation. Can you not impress this upon shipping authorities?"

It is estimated that at one time the A.E.F. had in use 294 different makes and body types of motor vehicles, 213 of which were produced in the U. S. In the repair shops and motor pools, supply officers tried to keep track of almost 60,000 separate and non-interchangeable spare parts, not to mention additional thousands of nuts, bolts, screws and cotter keys. It was the price paid for the failure to prepare—but it was not an unusual condition. After all, horses had

These massive, angry-looking Macks gave the appearance of being "at home" on a battleground. There was no mistaking these motorized brutes, and as a result, they were the sentimental favorites of many doughboys. The tankers shown here were photographed near Essey, France, just five days after the Armistice was signed.

U. S. Signal Corps Photo in The National Archives

Pennsylvania Historical and Museum Commission, Harrisburg

(Above) Motorcycles, staff cars and giant trucks revolutionized military transportation in World War I. (Below) Doughboys gave the "bulldog" nickname to the ferocious-looking Mack AC which was in continuous production from 1915 to 1939. The distinctive motor bonnet made the Mack one of the era's most-remembered trucks.

been in the army since the Revolutionary War, and Pershing had to appeal just as desperately for them. No wonder he was taken aback when the War Department, in the late summer of 1918, suggested that motor transportation should be substituted for horses wherever possible.

Somebody at headquarters had finally gotten Captain Williams' message!

In 1918 American manufacturers produced 227,250 trucks, and with shipping conditions improving, it appeared that General Pershing would finally get all the vehicles he needed. Fortunately, the Armistice provided the best possible solution, although new dilemmas were soon to devel-

Washington State National Guard

Washington State National Guard

(Above) Literally dozens of truck manufacturers got army contracts during and after World War I and adapted vehicles for military use. This rugged model had neither windshield nor headlights, an indication that driver comfort was little considered. (Below) A lineup of army veterans in Philadelphia after the war.

op. November 11, however, marked the end of the developmental era for trucks. Irving B. Babcock in his book "20 Years' Progress in Commercial Motor Vehicles" wrote that "World War I was the cradle in which the motor truck was nurtured." More realistically, it was the period in which motorized transport earned its "first pair of long pants."

Horseless Age editorialized in 1918: "This war has advertized the motor truck to the world more than anything else ever could." Infancy and adolescence had been left behind; the industry had come of age.

Before the war ended, efforts toward standardization began to pay off. The Quartermaster had developed the Standard B heavy truck, a non-commercial model which was often referred to by doughboys as the "Liberty." Before the Armistice, some 8,000 of them had been shipped overseas. Meanwhile, a smaller White had been designated as the army's Standard A model, winning the French Croix de Guerre for its services. The

Pennsylvania Historical and Museum Commission, Harrisburg

American Trucking Associations, Inc.

Post-war guardsmen from Cleveland felt every bump in the road when they traveled in this Model 20 White with solid tires fore and aft. Unlike his World War I predecessor, the driver had the luxury of a windshield.

Four Wheel Drive and the Nash Quad (formerly the Jeffery) were extremely effective in war-torn France. The "Bulldog" Mack, so named by the American serviceman because of its fierce-looking motor hood, was a special favorite because of its unusual appearance.

The war was a teamwork affair, and the entire trucking industry cooperated, including Henry Ford, who had had some earlier thoughts contrariwise. Now, new problems faced the manufacturers: What to do with production facilities geared to war-time needs? What to do about the thousands of war-surplus trucks which were certain to be a glut on the market?

Like America in general, the automotive industry set about the task of returning to a peace-time economy. But for truck manufacturers particularly, there was no "normalcy" to return to. Before the war, development was touch-and-go as scores of truck-builders plotted against the horse and not against one another. World War I had eliminated horses and mules from the competition, so the Armistice, in effect, signalled the beginning of an industrial war which was to leave a mounting toll of financial victims in its swath.

General Nelson Appleton Miles (1839-1925) lived to see his prediction come true. The "next war" *had* proved the value of the motor truck. Now the question was: How would it fare in peace-time?

Pennsylvania Historical and Museum Commission, Harrisburg

The demand for trucks in World War I was so great that standardization became a secondary factor. Nash Quads, "Bulldog" Macks and FWDs retained their individual appearances. Most other vehicles—like the one at the left—were known by doughboys as "Liberty trucks."

The Boeing Company

Aviation and the trucking industry shared the same period of development, being given impetus by World War I. This photo was taken in 1922 and shows an MB-3A pursuit plane being hauled from the Boeing airplane plant to a railroad siding in Seattle for shipment to the U. S. Army. Sitting in the spare tire of the White truck was E. N. Gott, one of three founders of the Boeing Airplane Company, which was to play a greater role in future wars.

Historical Collection, Title Insurance and Trust Company, San Diego

The Jeffery Quad (later Nash) was introduced in 1913 by Thomas B. Jeffery & Company. The four-wheel-drive principle made it extremely valuable as a military vehicle, as the army mule (in background) began his exodus.

AKRON TO BOSTON EXPRESS
GOOD YEAR
BOSTON, MASS.
AKRON
MIAMI FLA
NEW ORLEANS LA.
SHIP BY TRUCK

(Opposite page) The Goodyear Tire & Rubber Company

(Above) Michigan State Highway Department

Crews like this (including the young kibitzers in the rock wagon) were responsible for much of America's road-building before World War I. Engineering was not such an important factor because the demands of high-speed traffic had not yet arisen. Horses were still kings of the road when this picture was taken in Kalkaska County, Michigan.

When Roads Were Ridiculous

IN 1912 A BRITISH JOURNALIST wrote: "In the United States, roads as they are known in the Old World exist only within the purlieus of the well-established cities. Once beyond these boundaries, the highway gives way to an ill-defined track, full of holes, with its surface a stratum of treacherous dust, inches in thickness in summer and little more than a quagmire and pools of slime in the wet weather. Many of the roads upon the American continent are nothing more than trails, beaten down by the feet of the pack trains and the wheels of the prairie schooners of the pioneers in the western treks to find new lands of promise."

(Opposite page) Flimsy bridges which would support a horse and buggy often gave way under the weight of motor trucks. (Right) A transcontinental run in 1918 consisted of one obstacle course after another—with endless ruts, boulders, washouts and mudholes. The truck shown here was demonstrating the practicability of Goodyear pneumatic tires on a trip from Boston to San Francisco.

Unfortunately, his negative description was all too true!

As the historic cliche goes, America's roads were built on meandering Indian trails. In colo-

The Goodyear Tire & Rubber Company

Michigan State Highway Department

This was road-building the hard way, with teams, scoops and drags. The primitive construction methods generally resulted in primitive highways which were unsuited to the coming motor age.

Mud—everlasting mud—was the curse of the pioneer trucker. From coast to coast it came in a wide range of colors, viscosity and depth to test the mettle of drivers and their vehicles.

Virginia Department of Highways

nial days this was an interesting, if not romantic, solution to a basic need. The fact that the Indian trail philosophy was carried to a ridiculous extreme had a considerable effect on the development of trucks and trucking in the U. S.

In the beginning, automobiles and commercial vehicles were extremely limited by the roads of the period. Only the courageous—or the foolhardy—would venture outside the city limits in a horseless carriage of any type. As a matter of fact, it was usually possible to sink axle-deep in mud right in the middle of Main Street.

Needless to say, the situation demanded a whole new concept of road-building, and the advent of the automobile provided the sputtering catalyst which—years later—ultimately resulted in the nation's modern arterials.

America's highways date back to such early innovations as corduroy roads and "private capital" turnpikes. Most were little more than cleared byways, with cobblestones and planking being used but rarely on city streets. Then, in the early 1800s, two engineers in Great Britain turned the emphasis in road-building to hard-surfaces. Thomas Telford, who had been apprenticed to a stone mason, developed a layered system, beginning with large blocks of stone which, in turn, were covered with broken stone and then gravel. At the same time John Loudon MacAdam, a Scotsman who had saved a small fortune while working in his uncle's counting house in New York, returned to his homeland to buy a country estate. Becoming a road trustee in his district, he was appalled by the conditions which existed and promptly began a series of experiments in roadmaking. By 1815, as surveyor general of the Bristol roads, he was able to put his theories into practice. Surfacing of his roads consisted of broken stones, from 2 to 2½ inches in diameter, spread one foot thick on a prepared roadbed which was higher in the middle than at the edges. No loose earth or large stones were permitted. The initial binding material consisted merely of the dust and small particles of rock chipped off by the wheels of the coaches using the roads. In time a bitumen binder was added to the process which has found a lasting place in the English language as "macadam."

The first macadamized road in the United States was the Lancaster Turnpike between Philadelphia and Lancaster, Pennsylvania. Meanwhile, the federal government—using its constitutional authority "to establish post roads"—began to subsidize the so-called National Road between the

King County (Washington) Engineer

Even when concrete and other hard-surfaced roads became more and more commonplace, such deficiencies as tight curves, narrow width and lack of shoulders created accidents. Increased speed was an obvious contributing factor.

Truck drivers approached untested bridges with trepidation, and sometimes their fears were justified. A Boston-San Francisco run by a Goodyear experimental model, circa 1918, demonstrated the shabby condition of the nation's highways.

The Goodyear Tire & Rubber Company

King County (Washington) Engineer

(Above) This was a major road south of Seattle, Washington, but it could have been Anyplace, U. S. A., in the early days of automotive travel. (Below) A war-surplus truck, converted into a road-oil distributor, rescued this touring car from an Idaho ditch in an era when motorists were just beginning to feel their oats.

Potomac and Mississippi Rivers. For more than three decades—from 1806 to 1837—federal money was used in the gradual development of this early highway. Then, in the latter year, the responsibility for road-building was shifted to the states.

Strangely enough, it was the Bicycle Era—beginning about 1870—which generated America's first "good roads" movement. The League of American Wheelmen, from which evolved the American Road Builders Association, began a pressing campaign, causing President Benjamin Harrison to establish the U. S. Office of Road

Arthur C. Waller Collection

Inquiry in 1893. The basic legislation read in part: "To enable the Secretary of Agriculture to make inquiries in regard to the system of road management throughout the United States, to make investigations in regard to the best methods of road-making, and to enable him to assist the agricultural colleges and experiment stations in disseminating information on this subject, ten thousand dollars."

That same year the first brick surface on a rural road in the U. S. was laid on a four-mile stretch of the Wooster Pike near Cleveland, Ohio. Also in 1893 (as the Duryeas were preparing to introduce their original auto) the first concrete road was constructed in Bellefontaine, Ohio. Eleven years later the second concrete pavement was poured on Eagle Street in Le Mars, Iowa.

In 1904, when they were completing the Le Mars job and scoring the surface in four-inch squares "to protect horses from slipping," there were only 18 miles of bituminous rural roads in the nation (all in Massachusetts and Ohio) and less than five miles of the concrete variety. Altogether there were some 2,151,379 miles of public roads, almost half of which had not had improvements of any kind. Of the remainder, a thin layer of gravel constituted the only surfacing. Dr. H. Nelson Jackson, a surgeon from Burlington, Vermont, had focused national attention on this neglect a year earlier when he and a chauf-

King County (Washington) Engineer

Mountain roads were particularly hazardous for pioneer motorists who ventured off the cobblestones and the macadam. On the Sunset Highway in Washington State's Cascade Mountains, this tree presented a mental hazard, to say the least.

The rickety bridges of the early 1900s were simply not built to accommodate automobiles and trucks—but drivers crossed them just the same, hoping that they would bear up. This particular tragedy was caused by a flood washout.

King County (Washington) Engineer

Ray Beauchamp

From the very beginning, automobile accidents have always attracted the morbid curious. This scene was a harbinger of things to come, with a giant billboard advertising Red Crown gasoline and Zerolene motor oil to the motorists who chugged by to see what had befallen a fellow driver on the tight, flat curve.

feur drove his Winton touring car from San Francisco to New York City in 63 days, the first transcontinental run in history. It was eight years later before the first cross-country trip was made by a truck (see Page 38). Following Doctor Jackson's historic jaunt, numerous other group tours and individual junkets added to the growing interest in inter-state travel. Drivers who made it through the muck and mire became exponents of more and better roads. There weren't enough of them, however, and the Brownlow-Latimer Federal Good Roads Bill—the first of its kind ever to be introduced in Congress—died in committee in 1903.

During the ensuing decade, motor trucks began to appear in gradually increasing numbers. It became quite obvious that roads and bridges built for horses and bicycles would never do for five-ton hard-tired juggernauts. Still, there were not enough of them to force the issue. Between 1903

Old Dobbin had his troubles, but he somehow managed to stay on the road more than the new-fangled autos. As speed rates climbed, simple accidents turned into tragedies.

Ray Beauchamp

Sometimes it didn't take much to overturn a top-heavy truck. A wheel on a narrow or soft shoulder was enough to cause accidents like this one.

Ray Beauchamp

King County (Washington) Engineer

Underpasses, which seemed so adequate in the early 1920s, rapidly became obsolete. Many were so low and so narrow that truckers often found it difficult—if not impossible—to overcome these man-made obstacles.

King County (Washington) Engineer

America's expansive highway network did not just blossom overnight. In fact, the builders couldn't keep up with the automobiles as long as wheelbarrows continued to play a major role in road construction.

and 1910 the entire truck production in the nation amounted to 10,374 vehicles. In 1911, however, 10,655 trucks were built, and from then on the population of commercial vehicles spiraled. The following table indicates just what happened in the ten years which followed:

	Truck Production		Truck Production
1912	22,000	1917	128,157
1913	23,500	1918	227,250
1914	25,375	1919	316,364
1915	74,000	1920	322,039
1916	90,000	1921	147,550

In 1914, as World War I erupted in Europe and truck production began to soar in the U. S., this is what the hard-surfaced rural road picture looked like from coast to coast:

Bituminous mixtures	10,500 miles
Concrete	2,348 miles
Brick	1,600 miles
Bituminous concrete	(negligible)

That amounted to less than 15,000 total miles of hard-top highways, a situation which made some sort of action imperative.

It came finally in 1916 when there were some 3,600,000 trucks and autos driving on U. S. roads—or mired in them. On July 11 that year President Woodrow Wilson signed the Federal Aid Road Act (the Tice Law), the first legislation drafted to establish a nation-wide system of interstate highways. The act provided for the construction of rural public roads and defined them as "any public road over which the United States mails now are or may hereafter be transported." It called for federal matching funds up to 50 per cent for highway construction, but, more important, it insisted upon the creation of state highway departments to administer building programs—or no federal money would be forthcoming. By 1919 all 48 states were in the road business, and the stage was set for the development of a true network of roads rather than willy-nilly byways.

Up till this time it was possible to drive on a

New Hampshire Highway Department

New Hampshire used war-surplus trucks in 1920 to tackle the difficult task of modernizing her highways for a new era. The same scene was repeated in virtually all of the other 47 states.

Oregon State Highway Department

(Above) Between Salem and Jefferson, Oregon, a cab-less "Bulldog" Mack delivered a load of road mix which would have strained several teams of horses. (Below) World War I trucks were converted into dozens of practical, sometimes unique, road-building vehicles. This righthand-drive Pierce-Arrow became a road-oil distributor in Idaho.

fairly good road to a state border and then drop off into a mudhole as one crossed the line. This catch-as-catch-can system made impossible such traveling niceties as road maps. The Indian trail and cow path philosophy was at its end as the states submitted five-year plans for highway development to be coordinated by the federal government.

World War I was seriously disruptive of the new plan as the national interest was focused upon other things. In January of 1918 a 2.55-mile stretch of road between Richmond and the Alameda County line in California was opened, the first such project completed under the Federal Aid Road Act. The federal government contributed $24,244.56 of the $53,938.85 total. By Octo-

Arthur C. Waller Collection

ber of 1920 only 191 miles of mutually financed highways were ready for traffic.

Meanwhile, an unusual example of American enterprise marked the period. In 1912 Carl G. Fisher, founder of the Prest-O-Lite Company, proposed that automotive industry leaders sponsor the construction of a hard-surfaced transcontinental road which he suggested might be called the Coast-to-Coast Rock Highway. Fisher was an important pioneer in the industry, having conceived the idea of compressing carbide gas to provide early trucks and autos with headlights.

The dynamic industrialist, who in 1909 was co-founder of the Indianapolis Speedway, wrote to Editor Elbert Hubbard: ". . . the highways of America are built chiefly of politics, whereas the proper material is crushed rock, or concrete. We believe one magnificent highway of this kind, in

Tank trucks and a variety of other interesting conversions were made out of vehicles released from military service. Sometimes they were strictly jerry-built, like "Sloppy Sue" (second from top), a road-oil distributor consisting of a corrugated steel culvert mounted on an FWD. It was a familiar sight on projects in northern Idaho.

Photo credits (from top clock-wise): Oregon State Highway Department, Arthur C. Waller Collection, Virginia Department of Highways, Virginia Department of Highways, Arthur C. Waller Collection.

Portland Cement Association

Unique hand-operated turntables were used on early concrete road-building jobs. Lack of room to maneuver made the devices necessary so batch trucks like this 1-ton Model T Ford could deliver their loads and then return in the direction from which they came. These jitneys were stripped to the bare essentials: no windshields, no lights, no cabs. Fayette County, Illinois, was the locale for this picture taken near Hagarstown in the mid-twenties.

actual existence, will stimulate as nothing else could the building of enduring highways everywhere that will not only be a credit to the American people but that will also mean much to American agriculture and American commerce."

While Fisher's proposal for a free-enterprise roadway was greeted with considerable enthusiasm, he was right about the politics. The name he had offered was rejected and others proposed. When the "Lincoln Memorial Highway" was suggested, Democrats objected and countered with the "Thomas Jefferson Highway." In time, however, Lincoln won out, and in 1913 an organization was formed to get on with the project.

The original aim of the Lincoln Memorial Highway Association was to complete the transcontinental road from New York to San Francisco by May 1, 1915, in time for the Panama-Pacific Exposition in the latter city. Unfortunately, this goal was too ambitious, though an estimated 15,000 autos did use the incomplete highway to motor to the festivities in California.

Portland Cement Association

(Left) An Autocar batch truck with pneumatic tires on the job in Clinton County, Iowa, in 1921. (Right) Even on a portable turntable, this driver wore his cap backwards, the universal symbol for automotive speed back in 1923 when he was photographed in Sumner County, Kansas.

Portland Cement Association

Portland Cement Association

Workmen in Sac City, Iowa, emptied cement bags from a hard-tired Wilcox into a spindly Model T Ford batch truck. The Wilcox trade name existed between 1910 and 1927. This picture was taken in 1920.

Numerous problems arose, not the least of which was the choice of the route. President Wilson and a delegation from Maryland and Delaware objected because the highway didn't terminate in the nation's capital. Much later, President Warren G. Harding was to complain because the road didn't go through his hometown of Marion, Ohio. In Southern California a great hue-and-cry was raised to bring the highway to Los Angeles, and in Utah officials refused to have anything to do with a route heading directly westward from Salt Lake City. They wanted it to angle to the southwest, to add considerably more mileage in their own state, before continuing on to Los Angeles.

In the end the bickering and confusion prevented the completion of the highway as it was originally intended. Still, the venture was a notable success. The association developed reams of publicity which, in turn, generated broad interest in good roads. Portland cement was selected as the favored surfacing, and that industry was prevailed upon to donate thousands of barrels of its product to the program. So-called "seeding"

(Below) An FWD war veteran continued its useful career building roads in Washington State. (Right) While trucks improved the efficiency of road-building, old-fashioned muscle-power was still necessary.

Washington State Department of Highways

State Highway Commission of Kansas

Idaho Department of Highways

In the early 1920s the roster of trucks employed on highway projects from coast to coast was a lengthy one as the great "shakedown" of makes and models was underway. A GMC, one of the few survivors, carried a load of construction workers in Idaho. Thanks to the hard tires, they felt every rock in the road.

stretches of the highway were constructed in various states. Willys-Overland and General Motors subsidized sections of the road in Nevada and Wyoming. Though the 1915 target date came and went, the association continued its work with vigor.

In the summer of 1919, the Army Transport Corps got into the act. It decided to send a military motor truck convoy from Washington, D. C., to San Francisco, following generally the route of the Lincoln Memorial Highway. The convoy consisted of 300 enlisted men and officers, manning 65 trucks and other vehicles. There were two commercial trucks in the convoy, carrying a load of Firestone tires to that company's San Francisco branch. Colonel Charles W. McClure commanded the motor train; with him was an energetic young officer named Dwight D. Eisen-

Also in Idaho, this pioneer Pierce-Arrow, loaded with oil, had to be towed by a grader every time the road had an appreciable rise. Such deficiencies signalled the ultimate demise of the aging models.

Arthur C. Waller Collection

hower. The cross-country run — the first by a truck caravan of that size—took more than two months, during which time news coverage beamed still another spotlight on the need for adequate roads in general and the Lincoln Highway in particular.

No question about it, the national interest was aroused. The U. S. Bureau of Public Roads was created in 1918. That same year there was a concerted effort to relieve the railroads of some of the burdens of war-time shipping. Eighteen thousand trucks were driven into Baltimore, for ultimate overseas shipment, over routes selected by parties of engineers and maintained year-around by state and local authorities. In 1921 a second Federal Highway Act more clearly defined the aid program to develop a gigantic national road network. The Kahn-Wadsworth bill made possible the distribution of more than 25,000 surplus army trucks and other equipment to state highway departments for road-building purposes. Near Dyer, Indiana, the United States Rubber Company invested in a so-called "Ideal Section" of road on the Lincoln Highway, a 1⅓-mile stretch of lighted and landscaped pavement which was used as a model for concrete roads throughout the country. When finally completed, it consisted of four-lanes on a 110-foot right-of-way.

America's roadways had progressed amazingly in a few short years, but one stark truth emerged in the process: The job would never end!

Portland Cement Association

In 1920 war-surplus trucks were used in Illinois to test concrete, asphalt and brick roads. Carrying from five to 15 tons, the trucks pounded back and forth across 63 different experimental sections to determine the effects of heavy vehicles and steady traffic on types of paving materials. This so-called Bates Road Test was an indication of the growing interest in new and better roads.

In two decades White trucks had progressed considerably from the original steamer of 1900. Nine years later the company made its first gas model, and during World War I 18,000 Whites served the allied forces. After 1918 surplus vehicles were assigned throughout the nation, building roads which other generations of Whites would use.

Arthur C. Waller Collection

OHIO
1916
153882

(Opposite page) The Goodyear Tire & Rubber Company

North Dakota State Historical Society

The first delivery truck in Williston, North Dakota, was a two-cylinder Buick. Many of the early-day car manufacturers built trucks. Some—like White, Four Wheel Drive, and Diamond T—shifted entirely to trucks, while others—including Buick, Cadillac and Packard—later concentrated on automobiles.

They Came in All Shapes and Sizes

When the first commercial vehicle contest was held in New York in the spring of 1903, the trucks which appeared looked like the science fiction of another era.

With little precedent to follow—other than the horse-drawn vehicles of the past—builders of the revolutionary new power wagons drew upon their imaginations for design features and concepts of power. Like the contemporary author of their age, Jules Verne, they groped into the future for ideas which ranged from brilliant to downright impractical.

It was a period of great experimentation, the kind which could be fussed over in any basement, warehouse, tool shed, blacksmith shop or livery stable. In the beginning, little capital was necessary. Young mechanics with ambitious dreams made or scrounged the parts and pieces which

(Opposite page) Truck-tractors, forerunners of the modern semis, were experimented with well before World War I. This tri-wheeled model operated in Ohio in 1916. (Right) Before the turn of the century, J. W. Walters invented a unique three-wheeler which was manufactured briefly by the International Motor Wheel Company of New York. It was driven by a small gas motor mounted on the front wheel. It was an interesting idea, but it lacked the horsepower to make it practical.

Trailmobile, Inc.

they needed. Many of them labored in dark secrecy—some fearful that their magnificent ideas would be stolen, others dreading the negative reactions of neighbors, relatives and friends.

No wonder, then, that the finished products came rolling out as unlike as all the creatures on Noah's Ark. Each was an individual concept, with the "borrowing" limited simply because the entire automotive industry was in the embryonic stage.

There were, of course, the wagon-builders and the bicycle-makers who had a small head-start. Among the men whose names ultimately appeared on truck chassis, Colonel George Pope of Hartford, Connecticut, was the largest manufacturer of bicycles in the country; John and Horace Dodge developed a ball-bearing bicycle and established the Evans & Dodge Bicycle Company; Thomas B. Jeffery's company produced Rambler bicycles long before it made Rambler autos and Jeffery trucks.

John Mohler Studebaker and his brothers were famous wagon-makers. Charles W. Nash was a trimmer for the Durant-Dort Carriage Company; he and his employer—J. Dallas Dort—both later lent their names to motor trucks. The Mack brothers built wagons; so did George A. Brockway.

Thus it was that the earliest autos and commercial vehicles drew on the past for wagon boxes, artillery wheels, carriage brakes, crude axles and other existing components. That's why

The trucks below were typical of the unusual shapes and sizes which showed up on America's streets and highways during the first years of motorized transportation. The crude Sturgis (right) was a juggernaut of huge proportions which obviously fascinated lots of people—both young and old—in Los Angeles in 1905.

(Both photos) Automobile Manufacturers Association, Inc.

Los Angeles County Museum of History

they were called horseless carriages, power wagons and motor vans. After all, the pioneer builders had to start somewhere!

As a consequence, their creations came in all shapes and sizes. Standardization was an unknown consideration. Trucks, which were born of trial-and-error, had to be improved and refined in the cruel-and-clinical laboratory of competition The only other choice was oblivion.

It would be impossible to chronicle the lengthy list of successes and failures which marked the early years of the truck industry. A sampling, however, will more than suffice to show the chuckholes on the rough road of survival.

(Right) More of a locomotive than a truck, this electric tractor was used to shift freight cars for the Pennsylvania Railroad in Jersey City. It sported Kelly-Springfield blocks, a style of hard tire which was particularly popular in prepneumatic days.

(Right) Kelly-Springfield Tire Company

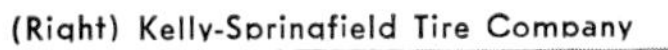

Truck and Coach Division, General Motors Corporation

One of the unusual features of the Grabowsky Power Wagon was its so-called removable power plant. The entire motor pulled out at the front like a bureau drawer. The company's advertising shouted long and loud about this innovation which made repairs and adjustments a simple, standup task. With a Grabowsky, it was not necessary "to get out and get under," as songwriters Grant Clarke and Edgar Leslie later penned in 1913.

Max Grabowsky boasted mechanical perfection in his trucks back in 1902 when the industry was in swaddling clothes. From the beginning his firm fought hard for business and kept alive while other pioneer manufacturers came and went, sometimes before they could get more than one or two vehicles on the market.

WILLIAM CRAPO DURANT was without peer as a salesman, promoter and manipulator in the pioneer days of the automotive industry.

He was born in Boston in 1861, but soon after his family moved to Flint, Michigan, thus setting the stage for the amazing career which was to follow.

As a youngster, he sold groceries, labored in his grandfather's lumber mill and clerked in a drug store. In the latter role he became acquainted with patent medicines and promptly went on the road as a salesman for exotic cure-alls. After that, he sold cigars, then insurance, then real estate.

When he was in his mid-twenties, he teamed with Josiah Dallas Dort, a young hardware clerk, to establish the Durant-Dort Carriage Company. Their success was phenomenal, and with the advent of the motor age, Super-salesman Durant was ready for new worlds to conquer.

David Dunbar Buick, who perfected a car with

Max Grabowsky, shown in the cab of a refurbished 1915 GMC, was one of the trucking industry's earliest pioneers. In 1902 he was producing the forerunners of General Motors trucks, first under the Grabowsky name and then as the Rapid Motor Vehicle Company.

Truck and Coach Division, General Motors Corporation

Automobile Manufacturers Association, Inc.

Teamsters of another era loaded sizable cargoes of beer on a pair of Rapid trucks. This was during the early anti-horse period when a typical Rapid advertisement read: "Waiting for the other fellow is a losing game. To continue the archaic, inhuman, expensive method of transporting merchandise with horses is the height of foolishness."

a valve-in-head engine, organized the Buick Motor Car Company in 1903. Unfortunately (like several other pioneers of the industry), Buick could make automobiles, but he couldn't sell them. A year later William Durant had control of the firm. The 1903 production of Buicks had been a mere 16 cars; in the panic year of 1907, Durant sold almost 2,300.

This merely whetted his appetite. On September 16, 1908, he chartered the General Motors Company in New Jersey, and in the ensuing two

In 1911 the Pioneer Commercial Auto Company was offering Brockway delivery wagons and Reliance trucks to its customers in Los Angeles. That same year the General Motors Truck Company was formed, with the Reliance Truck Company included in the combination.

Los Angeles County Museum of History

Truck and Coach Division, General Motors Corporation

By the mid-twenties semi-trailers began to appear more and more frequently on U. S. highways. Smith Trucking Company of Detroit hauled Buick auto bodies in this van towed by a GMC. By this time the driver had the protection of a windshield, but a rear-view mirror was a virtually unheard of luxury. To check clearance on his left before making a turn, the driver either craned his neck or hoped for the best. Accidents were simply occupational hazards.

years he acquired control of Oldsmobile, Cadillac, Oakland, Welch, Elmore, Ewing, Marquette, Rainier and several other auto producers and parts manufacturers. Included in the package were the firms which built the Reliance, Cartercar and Rapid trucks.

The Cartercar actually originated in the Michigan State Prison where Byron T. Carter, superintendent of the machine shop, had the first model made by prison labor. Several years later —in 1910—Carter was fatally injured when he stopped to help a woman motorist whose auto had stalled. The crank kicked back as Carter was trying to start the engine, striking him in the jaw. The case portrays vividly an occupational hazard which pioneer truckers knew well!

The Rapid truck was a re-name of the Grabowsky power wagon first built by Max and Morris Grabowsky in 1900. They sold their first truck two years later under their own name. Ultimately, their firm became the Rapid Motor Vehicle Company of Pontiac, Michigan. The Rapid truck had a favorable performance record, including its successful participation in several Glidden tours. An advertisement in 1910 said: "There are many derelicts of other makes, but none of the Rapid." That same year the name disappeared because of the business maneuver.

Fading with it (at least temporarily) was William Durant. He had let his interest in empire-building over-ride the profit-and-loss statement, and General Motors tottered on the brink of financial disaster. Durant lost control to a combine of bankers which replaced him with Charles W. Nash.

Historical Collection, Title Insurance and Trust Company, San Diego

The Chevrolet Motor Car Company was organized in 1911 by William Crapo Durant to produce automobiles designed by Louis Chevrolet, a French-Swiss mechanic and a racing driver for Buick. Durant used the company to regain control of General Motors in 1915, retaining the Chevrolet name for both trucks and automobiles.

Seattle Historical Society (James P. Lee Collection)

In 1919 the GMC insignia was already well known. Equally recognizable was the uniquely shaped radiator which identified Packard trucks and automobiles during that era. This photo was taken in Seattle after World War I. J. F. Duthie & Company owned the GMC, while the Packard belonged to the Fisher Flouring Mills Company.

In 1911, the new organization created the General Motors Truck Company, combining in it all commercial vehicle production. The result was a new line of GMC trucks, as Cartercar, Reliance and Rapid faded into historical oblivion. The firm produced both gasoline and electric models ranging in size from one-half to six tons.

GMC trucks, like those of other manufacturers, played a vital role in World War I. Meanwhile, William C. Durant was back in the picture. Following his 1910 demise, he had formed the Chevrolet Motor Company to make an automobile designed by Louis Chevrolet. Under Durant's direction and salesmanship, the firm grew so rapidly that in September of 1915, he devised one of the greatest financial coups in automotive history: his Chevrolet organization gobbled up General Motors Company. He remained at the helm of GMC until another financial crisis toppled him after World War I. Meanwhile, in 1918 General Motors Corporation was organized as the over-all parent company, rectifying the unusual situation in which the whole (GMC) was owned by one of its parts (Chevrolet).

GMC and Chevrolet trucks remained among the narrowing list of survivors. Durant, the indomitable, turned his talents to the development and sales of Flint, Star and Durant autos, as well as Mason trucks. He had ridden a gigantic roller-coaster of success and failure, ending in a downhill run.

Automobile Manufacturers Association, Inc.

Sightseeing buses were built by a number of early-day truck manufacturers. The Rapid Motor Vehicle Company advertised that open-air models like this one would "pay for themselves in one season" at country clubs, hotels and summer resorts.

Mack Trucks, Inc

Commercial vehicles bearing the Mack name date back to 1900 when a 20-passenger bus was built. In the following year the Mack brothers produced several gas-operated trucks in their Brooklyn wagon shop. By 1905 they had outgrown the original plant, so operations were shifted to Allentown, Pennsylvania. In the company's first decade, it produced trucks, like the one above, ranging from 2 to 7½ tons, discarding experimental steam and electric models.

Mack

On March 14, 1924, 60-year-old John M. Mack was hurrying to Weatherley, Pennsylvania, in his stylish Chandler coupe. A tragic few moments later he was dead, victim of a collision with a trolley car on the Lehigh Valley Transit line.

It was ironic that an automobile should be the cause of Jack Mack's death, for he had given a quarter of a century of his life to the creation and perfection of motor vehicles.

Young Mack left school at the age of 14 and became a teamster for a construction crew. Later he went to sea as a stationary engineer on a Caribbean freighter, after which he accepted landlubber's employment with a Brooklyn wagonbuilder. In the late 1890s, he and his brother, Augustus, bought the business, and the prologue of the Mack story came to an end.

But the saga itself was just beginning!

Three other brothers — Charles, Joseph and William — were variously associated with the wagon shop, but the guiding hand and the mechanical genius behind the struggling new company belonged largely to Jack Mack. Before the

Public Relations Archives, Texaco, Inc.

Carriage lights, a squeeze-bulb horn and righthand drive were features of this vintage Mack tank truck. While some of the earliest trucks were guided by a tiller, the Mack brothers used a steering wheel in their original bus and all succeeding models.

turn of the century, the firm was building bodies for horseless carriages, and Jack was experimenting with ideas for both electric and steam vehicles. It is probable that he discussed such matters with his friend, John P. Holland, inventor of the first submarine sold to the U. S. Navy. Finally, in 1900, the Mack brothers—using one of Jack's designs—assembled a gas-operated open-air bus big enough to accommodate 20 passengers.

This was the famous Mack No. 1 which was sold to Isaac Harris, who used it for sightseeing tours through Brooklyn's Prospect Park. Eight years later it was converted into a truck to serve a new owner until 1917. Meanwhile, eight more buses and trucks were built in 1901, as the Mack Brothers Motor Company succeeded the wagon factory.

By 1905 the new firm was growing out of its limited quarters. Joe Mack, then a silk merchant in Allentown, Pennsylvania, convinced his brothers that they should join him there. Like most of the pioneer truck and auto manufacturers, the Macks ultimately found themselves in a tight pinch for working capital. In 1911 a syndicate headed by the J. P. Morgan interests stepped into the picture. The Mack organization was merged with the Saurer Motor Company of Plainfield, New Jersey, the American licensee of the Swiss truck which just that year had made the first transcontinental crossing of the U. S. by a commercial vehicle. The new firm was named the International Motor Company.

Shortly thereafter, I. M. C. absorbed the Hewitt Motor Company of New York, manufacturers of both autos and trucks. Edward R. Hewitt, grandson of Peter Cooper (who built the "Tom Thumb," America's first steam locomotive, in 1830), had been trained as an engineer at Princeton and the University of Berlin. He left the family glue factory to build horseless carriages.

Hewitt objected to the financial maneuver, insisting that International Motor Company merely wanted his "superior" designs. His stockholders out-voted him, however, so he went along with the new arrangement as a consulting engineer. Later when further pecuniary difficulties plagued the company and the Mack title was restored to the firm's trucks, Hewitt again was incensed be-

Mack Trucks, Inc.

Artist Howard Nostrand, Jr., paintings of pioneer Mack trucks help preserve the history of one of the industry's oldest manufacturers. From top to bottom, the vehicles are a 1906 seat-over-engine, a 1907 7-ton dump truck, a 1911 fire engine and a 1913 2-ton panel.

Mack Trucks, Inc.

Mack's famous AC model was introduced in 1915 and manufactured—with improvements—until the advent of World War II. During that period the famous "Bulldog" was assigned every conceivable truck task. During World War I, for instance, a number of Macks were fitted out as degasser units to revive victims of gas attacks.

cause he felt his name should have been chosen.

Gradually these internal problems worked themselves out, and in 1915 the company unveiled a truck which was to shape its entire future. The vehicle was the AC model, the Mack "Bulldog," as it came to be known by the American doughboys in France. The "Bulldog" had a longer production life than Henry Ford's Model T, persisting until 1939. Like the "Tin Lizzie," it became an industry symbol. "Built like a Mack truck" caught on in the household idiom of the U. S.

Mack's World War I record gave the company the impetus to survive the doldrums of the early twenties. In addition to the popular "Bulldog," Mack built a line of fire engines which helped keep the firm solvent. This specialty dated back

This vintage Mack hauled freight of all kinds in Washington State's Puget Sound country. Pioneer trucker Leo F. Echelbarger established the firm which ultimately became Edmonds-Alderwood Auto Freight.

Ech's Burner Oils, Inc., Lynnwood, Washington

U. S. Signal Corps Photo in The National Archives

"Bulldog" Macks were prominent in the U. S. Army's first transcontinental convoy in 1919. In a rather un-military manner this vintage model boasted a banner which read: "We're off for Frisco!" A young officer named Dwight D. Eisenhower was a member of the convoy staff, gaining experience in truck logistics.

to 1909 when the firm produced an aerial ladder truck for the city of Allentown. Two years later it introduced the first of its highly efficient pumpers which helped hurry the horse out of the fire-fighting business.

Jack Mack and his brothers—like the Whites, the Dodges, the Grahams, the Stanleys, the Duryeas, the Studebakers and others—parlayed a family enterprise into a major automotive manufacturing company. Unlike the majority of the contemporary brother combinations, the Macks—and their trucks—had staying power!

Kenworth Motor Truck Company

The Gersix was largely an "assembled" truck, being put together from parts supplied by other manufacturers. It was first produced by the Gerlinger Motor Company in 1915 when the war in Europe was already beginning to create material shortages. The firm nearly folded when its source of axles disappeared.

IN A PERIOD when other truck manufacturers were withering away like pumpkins on a drought-stricken vine, a tiny company in Seattle, Washington, was just beginning to make itself known in the Pacific Northwest.

With thousands of surplus war trucks glutting the market, the early 1920s were definitely *not* the best years to get started in the commercial vehicle business. But no one slipped that hot tip to the officers of the Gersix Manufacturing Company in late 1922, so they went right ahead with their plans to re-organize their firm and introduce a new truck with a four-cylinder Buda engine.

Since the "six" in the original name was no longer appropriate, there was considerable discussion about what to call the new product. President William Gray ultimately solved the dilemma when he coined the word Kenworth from the names of two major stockholders: H. W. Kent and Edgar K. Worthington.

Both Kent and Worthington had begun their careers as junior clerks and had risen to important positions in the maritime industry. In time they were to transfer their years of experience to the struggling organization — Kenworth Motor Truck Corporation—which became an official entity on January 22, 1923. Worthington was named president and Kent first vice president.

Actually, the new company's ancestry dated

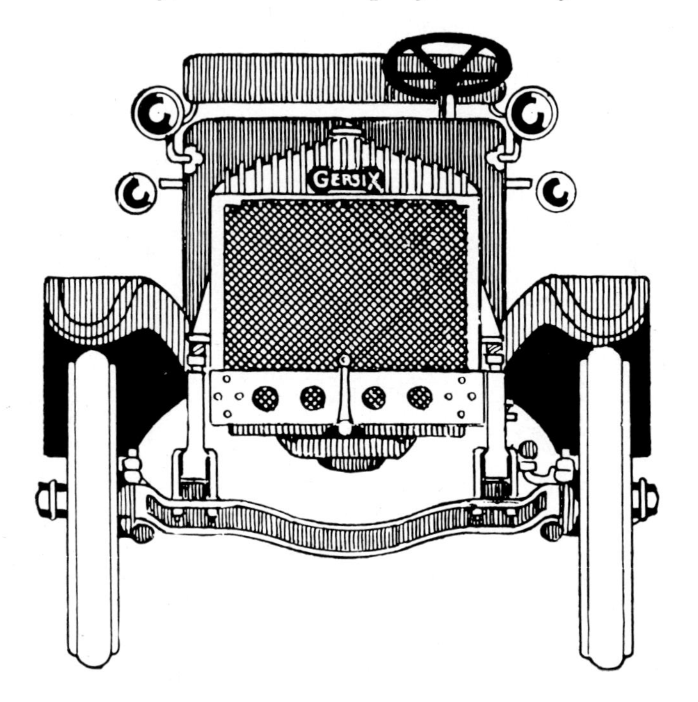

Kenworth Motor Truck Company

Kenworth Motor Truck Company

back to 1915 when the Gerlinger Motor Company was founded in Portland, Oregon, to build gas-powered trucks primarily for the logging industry. Like many other small truck-building operations, the Gerlinger firm sputtered along with not much promise. After a year it was shifted to Tacoma, Washington. In 1918—as the Gersix Manufacturing Company—it was moved northward again, this time to Seattle.

The original Gersix was basically an "assembled" truck as were many others in that period. Components were obtained from other manufacturers and put together to form the final product. The demands of World War I, however, indirectly started the company on its road to self-sufficiency when its axle supply was cut off and there was no other choice but to manufactre its own.

Gersix trucks in limited quantities came off a production line which one old-timer described as "two chalk marks on the floor where we placed the axles and then filled out in between." As a logging truck, though, the Gersix proved itself, and company salesmen sold all that could be made —taking in horses and harness as down-payments. Yet, the firm made little head-way in the difficult period following the war, so the re-organization

Truck manufacturing companies were comparatively rare in the western states. The Gersix was produced originally in Portland, Oregon, before World War I, and then later in Tacoma and Seattle, Washington. The model below is a pioneer dump truck with a steel box. Note the unusual rear wheels for driving in sand or soft ground.

Kenworth Motor Truck Company

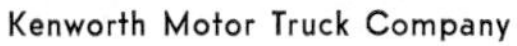

Kenworth Motor Truck Company

Kenworth Motor Truck Company

The Gersix (left) was a worm-drive truck with a six-cylinder motor. The first syllable of its name came from a contraction of Gerlinger. It was the forerunner of the Seattle-built Kenworth (right).

effort was made, and the Kenworth truck, as such, was born.

The new company was not an over-night sensation, producing only 78 trucks in its first year. But in 1923 a young engineer named John G. Holmstrom introduced a policy of custom-designing for each individual Kenworth which was to prove a vital factor in the firm's success. The idea of building a vehicle for a specific assignment was not new—but at Kenworth it was practiced as well as preached. Workmen began to refer to themselves as "truck tailors," a sure sign that the philosophy had caught on.

In 1924 production improved infinitesimally to 80 vehicles; a year later it had edged upward to 94. Not until 1927, however, did the company top the century mark when it completed 159 trucks. Once the milestone had been reached, a bright future dawned for the still young organization which had defied the business trends and prognostications of the post-war era.

Historically, Kenworth trucks appeared on the scene at the tag-end of the pioneer period. By then scores of manufacturers had come and gone as competition grew keener and survival-of-the-fittest became an industry keynote. The Kenworth story, however—with its Gersix prologue—is a vital part of the motor truck saga. It proved again that success is possible in spite of great odds . . . if conviction, quality and dedicated personnel have anything to do with it!

These were undoubtedly two of the first Kenworths, as the 1923 license plates would indicate. The company was incorporated in January of that year and the Gersix name dropped. The small firm produced 78 trucks in 1923. By comparison, in the same 12 months Ford factories turned out more than two million vehicles.

Kenworth Motor Truck Company

FWD Corporation

The enactment of prohibition in 1917 eliminated an important phase of the trucking industry—at least for a time. After World War I trucks were involved in the illegal, often dangerous, excitement of bootlegging. Not so this 3-ton Model B FWD, however, which was delivered to Binzel Brewery of Beaver Dam, Wisconsin, in 1913.

"WHO EVER HEARD of a mule walking on only two legs?"

With that question on his mind, Otto Zachow—the son of German immigrants—started work on an idea to develop an automobile with four-wheel-drive. The year was 1906, and by then, more than 700 patents had been granted for similar concepts: all unsuccessful!

But Otto Zachow, master blacksmith, didn't know about all those failures; he only knew that the horseless carriages of his day were virtually powerless in mud and loose sand—and he proposed to do something about it.

In Clintonville, Wisconsin, he operated a small machine shop with his brother-in-law, William A. Besserdich. Together they repaired steam engines, threshing machines and other broken-down devices which found their way to the forge and anvil of their tiny plant. They also became a sales agency for the Reo automobile, and the one-cylinder demonstration model they bought was the first car in Clintonville.

Reputedly taking an idea from the tumbling rods of an old-fashioned threshing machine, Zachow designed a mechanism which would permit him to deliver power to all four wheels of an

FWD Corporation

Victor Fremont Lawson, long-time publisher of the Chicago Daily News and president of the Associated Press from 1894 to 1900, was photographed with this new FWD which he bought in 1912.

auto and still steer it effectively. Immediately he journeyed to Fon du Lac, Wisconsin, where his son, Clarence, was serving an apprenticeship as a machinist and draftsman. For three days the father and son cloistered themselves in the local Palmer House as they laboriously transferred Otto's ideas onto paper.

In Clintonville Zachow sought the advice of Walter A. Olen, an attorney who would one day head the FWD organization, and patent applications were submitted. On March 24, 1908, the first of numerous patents were granted and the Zachow-Besserdich machine shop tackled a new project.

The two brothers-in-law devoted all their spare time to the construction of a car which would include Otto's ideas. They decided to make it a steamer, and *The Clintonville Tribune* reported that they lost valuable time when "an unscrupulous firm" sold them a poor boiler. A change was made, however, and on Saturday, December 26, 1908, they unveiled their new creation to the citizens of Clintonville.

A week later *The Tribune* noted: "With an ordinary dry goods box placed on the framework of the auto to answer the purpose of a seat, they have plowed through snowdrifts three feet deep, pushed huge billows ahead of them, gone over the roughest and most slippery roads and climbed the steepest hills to be found as well as to speed the machine up to a 25 mile hour clip and through it all, the newly patented mechanism of their four wheel drive has answered perfectly every demand made upon it."

FWD Corporation

Luella Bates, FWD's first woman demonstration driver, was greeted by officials of the New York Auto Show after she drove this 3-ton truck from Clintonville, Wisconsin, to Gotham in 1919.

The four-wheel-drive principle, proved during World War I, made the FWD a favored vehicle for off-the-road use. In California the Clintonville trucks were introduced to the sugar beet fields which offered less resistance than some of the roads over which earlier FWDs had operated before and during the war.

FWD Corporation

In spite of this glowing report, the steam engine did not satisfy the two craftsmen, so they rebuilt their auto, using a four-cylinder gasoline engine. They nicknamed their creation the "Battleship," and when it performed to their satisfaction, they formed the Badger Four Wheel Drive Auto Company on January 9, 1909. Joining them was Dr. William H. Finney, the local physician to whom they had sold their first Reo some two years earlier.

Creating a new auto and then producing it in quantity for market are two different problems. Neither the two blacksmiths nor their doctor partner were up to the second step, so their tiny company languished. Then Walter Olen, the young attorney who had received $3 for forwarding Zachow's initial applications to a patent attorney in Washington, D. C., stepped into the picture. The board of directors was increased, land was purchased for a factory, the "Badger" dropped from the company title and the construction of a dozen automobiles was scheduled. (Olen

FWD Corporation

This Model M was a far cry from the original FWD auto with which Otto Zachow and William A. Besserdich introduced their four-wheel-drive principle in 1908.

was to serve as president of the firm for more than four decades.)

Still, the company experienced no magic transformation, even though the converted FWD Scout Car and the Company's first two-ton model had succeeded well in U. S. Army tests. (See "America's Trucks Go to War," Page 49). In 1911 the company built and sold one car (to August Matuzucszak of Clintonville). In 1912 six automobiles and five trucks were produced. A year later five $1\frac{1}{2}$-ton trucks and 14 three-ton trucks rolled out of the factory.

It appeared that the big dream in the small

Near Placentia, California, this rugged FWD hauled steel casings to the oil fields. By the mid-twenties, heavy-duty trucks of all kinds were operating versatilely from coast to coast. Against the backdrop of history, the development was amazingly rapid; just a few years earlier skeptics insisted that motor vehicles could never succeed.

FWD Corporation

FWD Corporation

Stockholders and interested citizens of Clintonville, Wisconsin, gathered at the first factory of the Four Wheel Drive Auto Company in the pre-World War I period when dreams were big and sales were small. The firm began moving into this building on July 13, 1911, and the board of directors held its first meeting there the following day.

town would never materialize — and then the rumble of war hit the globe. FWD trucks were demonstrated before representatives of foreign nations, and on March 23, 1915, the English government placed an order for 50 trucks to be delivered in 40 days. Clintonville virtually exploded; in less than six weeks the local factory had to build more vehicles than it had in its entire history!

Despite complications, the company met the challenge. FWDs went to England and Russia, and follow-up orders were received. On November 26 the management gave 450 dressed geese to its employees, and in celebration the workers marched down Clintonville's main street with their Thanksgiving dinners dangling from their shoulders. The happy impromptu event has come to be known in local lore as the "Great Goose Parade."

FWD had passed the crisis. In 1916 the U. S. Quartermaster Corps ordered 147 three-ton Model Bs for Pershing's Punitive Expedition in Mexico. More rush orders came from Europe. Then, on March 18, 1917, 84 FWDs aboard the liner *Vigilancia* fell victim to a German torpedo. It was one of the acts which spurred the U. S. declaration of war less than one month later. By July the Clintonville company had a contract with the federal government calling for 3,750 trucks to be delivered at the rate of 175 a month. Under a patent license arrangement, FWDs were made for military use by the Peerless Motor Truck Company, Cleveland; Kissell Motor Car Company, Hartford, Wisconsin; Premier Motor Corporation of Indianapolis, and Mitchell Motors Company, Racine, Wisconsin. All in all, nearly 15,000 trucks—born of the pioneer labors of Otto Zachow and William Besserdich—were assigned to the war effort.

And what about the originators?

Zachow had resigned from the company back in 1910 so that he could devote more time to the repair work which had piled up in the machine shop. Besserdich sold out in 1914 and later established rival companies in Milwaukee and Oshkosh, Wisconsin, neither of which succeeded.

Meanwhile, FWD survived the post-war depression, using a national advertising campaign and women demonstration drivers. Otto Zachow's basic idea had been a good one, and the trucks which succeeded the historic "Battleship" continued to compete successfully in a new era.

International Harvester Company

In 1914 this jitney bus was made by converting a high-riding IHC Auto Wagon. The following year the company abandoned its original design, reducing the size of the wheels, increasing the engine to four cylinders and generally producing a more conventional vehicle. (Note the high button shoes on the boarding passenger.)

Cyrus Hall McCormick was the son of a Virginia farmer who failed in his efforts to invent a grain-cutting machine. Young Cyrus, however, took up where his father left off, and in 1831—at the age of 22—he built and successfully tested the reaper which was to win him an honored niche in agricultural history.

The McCormick Harvesting Machine Company which he established in Chicago ultimately became one of the nation's leading suppliers of farm equipment. In 1902—18 years after McCormick's death—the firm merged with its chief competitor

The original Auto Wagon developed by E. A. Johnston was a righthand-drive two cylinder high-wheeler. It was designed to help the farmer solve his farm-to-market transportation problems. Production of Auto Buggies and Auto Wagons got underway in 1907.

International Harvester Company

This painting depicts a typical happenstance in the pioneer days of trucking. The vehicle involved was an International Harvester Company Auto Wagon, introduced in 1907. Motor cars were still relatively scarce at the time, and horses were often unmanageable when the two modes of transportation shared the same street.

In the drawing the Auto Wagon seems to be traveling at a high rate of speed. The instruction folder which accompanied the early IHC models offered this bit of advice: "Caution! This machine is designed to be run at a maximum speed of 20 miles per hour. A higher rate of speed is dangerous and is injurious to the machine."

International Harvester Company

(Deering Harvester) and three smaller organizations to form the International Harvester Company. Its goal was to provide the machinery needed by farmers, not only in the United States, but throughout the civilized world.

By the turn of the century it was growing obvious that farm-to-market transportation would be a key factor in the advancement of agriculture. At that time, farmers who were not located near a railroad had to depend upon horse and wagon to haul their produce into town, an inadequate, time-consuming process. The advent of the horseless carriage hopefully offered an answer to their dilemma.

As early as 1898, E. A. Johnston of the McCormick firm's engineering department had installed a gas engine in a wagon-type chassis and had driven the resultant vehicle between his home and the factory for several months. Johnston, who also developed an auto-mower for the company in 1900, continued to improve his crude car, and by 1905 he completed an Auto Buggy at IHC's plant in Rock Falls, Illinois. It was designed to look as much as possible like the traditional horse-drawn vehicle after which it was named. It was operated by a two-cylinder, air-cooled engine—power enough for a farmer to haul moderate amounts of produce to market and to take his family to church on Sunday.

In the spring of 1907, 100 of these Auto Buggies were put into production in Chicago. Meanwhile, an Auto Wagon, with a little more carrying capacity, was also introduced. Both vehicles caught on, and the company developed an assem-

(Left) IHC officials of a later generation pose proudly with two pioneers of the firm's truck line. (Below) After World War I, International Harvester introduced its new "speed" truck, with radiator ahead of the engine and pneumatic tires instead of hard rubber. One of these models was the first four-wheeled stock model vehicle to cross the Sahara Desert. It was driven by Sir Charles Markham and Baron Bror Frederik von Blixen-Finecke.

(Both photos) International Harvester Company

International Harvester Company

In 1915, the same year the "Bulldog" Mack was unveiled, International Harvester came out with a new truck of its own, also with a unique motor bonnet. The model above (circa 1920) was a rugged vehicle totally unlike the Auto Wagon which preceded it. Internationals of this type had radiators located behind the engines.

bly line at its Akron Works to manufacture them in quantity.

IHC roadsters and touring cars came off E. A. Johnston's drawing board in 1908, and a decision was made to add them to the line. In 1910 and 1911, approximately 1,500 passenger autos were produced before the company abandoned the idea in order to concentrate entirely on trucks. The latter, it was concluded, were more in keeping with IHC's policy of helping the farmer with his transportation bottleneck.

The original Auto Buggies and Auto Wagons had purposely been made with high, narrow wheels in the belief that such a design would be most practical on the existing muddy, deep-rutted rural roads. With the improvement of highways, however, company engineers reduced the diameter of the wheels, and the International took on the appearance of the conventional trucks then on the market. The 1915 model had a unique snub-nosed motor bonnet which set it apart from most of its competitors. Only the Kelly-Springfield of that era was similar.

One of the new-type Internationals proved its capabilities on June 14, 1916, when it became the first truck to scale Pike's Peak. The timing couldn't have been better. The U. S. Army—with the help of a conglomerate fleet of motor trucks—had begun to chase Pancho Villa in Mexico just three months earlier. The warring nations of Europe were placing orders for more and more American vehicles. The International Harvester Company joined the challenging production effort and ultimately delivered thousands of trucks for World War I service.

In the post-war period when most companies were nervously looking for buyers and retrenching, International Harvester introduced a new pneumatic-tired "speed" truck and forged ahead. By 1925 the company proudly asserted that it was the nation's largest manufacturer of a complete line of commercial vehicles.

Cyrus McCormick would have been pleased with the progress!

International Harvester Company

This closed-cab worm-drive 1½-ton International was a notable improvement over most pre-World War I trucks. A model of this general type was the first to climb Pike's Peak, accomplishing the feat on June 14, 1916.

Harrah's Automobile Collection, Reno, Nevada

The White Company introduced tireless all-steel wheels for use in heavy hauling assignments. They worked satisfactorily on ideal ground, but the noble experiment failed when rocky roads virtually shook the trucks to pieces.

THE WHITE SEWING MACHINE COMPANY of Cleveland, Ohio, was a versatile organization. It first ventured into the transportation business when it produced roller skates and bicycles before the turn of the century. And when the horseless carriage fever swept the country, its contagion engulfed the three sons of Thomas H. White.

The latter was a wise father who didn't force bobbins and treadles on young Windsor, Walter and Rollin when they were more interested in steam engines and sprocket wheels. After all, since 1859 the elder White had been making and promoting the sewing machine he invented in his spare time while working in a Massachusetts chair factory. Now, forty years later, he agreed that the new generation deserved an opportunity to test its ideas just as he had.

It was Rollin White, an engineering graduate of Cornell University, who perfected a flash boiler for steam automobiles in 1899, an invention which was to give the early White cars an edge over most contemporaries. Windsor—also an engineer who had been working in the family plant since 1892—teamed with his brother to complete a vehicle for Rollin's new power unit to propel. Walter contributed, too, but as a law graduate, his interests were directed largely outside the factory to the organization of sales and customer service programs.

In 1900 the original White auto—an open-air Stanhope with wire wheels—was ready for testing. At the same time the brothers were working on a delivery van to introduce to the commercial

White Motor Corporation

The earliest White trucks were steam-driven, tiller-guided delivery vans. In 1902 they proved themselves with a perfect score in a 500-mile reliability run from New York to Boston and return. The company made its first gas truck in 1909.

Kenworth Motor Truck Company Collection

The logging industry really tested the mettle of trucks and truckers. Enormous weights and treacherous roads made the hauling of logs like these a stern test for both men and equipment. This teamster had side curtains and a celluloid windshield on his White—but he didn't allow much for visibility.

U. S. Post Office Department

This classic photo shows a White truck, circa 1914, adapted for parcel post deliveries. At the time it was the epitome of automotive progress, with headlights, pneumatic tires and a substantial windshield. The U. S. Post Office Department had experimented with motor vehicles before 1900, so its long record of truck usage has few challengers.

market. The following year Fred S. Borton of Cleveland bought the first car, and the sewing machine company was launched on a new career.

By 1902 the Whites had produced a five-ton truck with a steam stack like a railroad locomotive. That same year two of the delivery vans and three Stanhopes participated successfully in a 500-mile reliability run from New York City to Boston and back. Customers soon replaced the skeptics!

The White brothers—as did Henry Ford and other manufacturers—took advantage of public test runs and speed races to prove the capabilities of their products. In England, Walter White captured the honors in a 650-mile road trial. At home White steamers performed outstandingly on tours from New York to Pittsburgh and from New York to St. Louis. In 1905 "Whistling Billy," a White racer, established a new world's record for a mile: 48 3/5 seconds.

The emergence of gas-driven autos and trucks signalled the ultimate demise of steamers, in spite of their early successes. Fortunately, the Whites were alert to the change, and in 1909 they produced their first gas vehicles.

In less than a decade the concept of motor-

Public Relations Archives, Texaco, Inc.

Following meritorious service in World War I, White trucks returned to peace-time tasks. The petroleum industry, expanding to fill the needs of a nation on wheels, used thousands of trucks, many of them "war veterans."

ized transport had gone from untested theory to proven reality. From the beginning, White trucks were in the vanguard of this rapid development; the ensuing ten years would be even more amazing in terms of automotive progress.

A 1½-ton White participated successfully in the historical 1,509-mile U. S. Army test of 1912. That same year, trucks from the Cleveland company served American troops at Ching Wan Too in North China. Concurrently, Czar Nicholas of Russia witnessed competitive tests, and promptly ordered ten three-ton Whites, the largest foreign sale of American-made trucks up till that time.

In 1913 Whites went to Haiti and Santo Domingo with U. S. servicemen; in 1914 they were in Vera Cruz, Mexico, with General Frederick Funston and in pursuit of Pancho Villa with General John J. Pershing. Before the United States declared war on Germany, great fleets of White trucks were serving the French Army. In 1918 thousands of Whites were with the A.E.F. as the official Class A standard truck of the U. S. Army. That same year, the company discontinued making passenger cars.

The pioneer saga of The White Company spans the history of trucking. It is an international story, too, as White vehicles saw unusual service throughout the world. In 1907 Walter C. White organized a convoy of his company's trucks in Los Angeles to speed relief supplies to the victims of the San Francisco earthquake and fire. That same year Whites were on duty in Jamaica during a similar tragedy. They helped feed thousands of starving people in the Near East in 1917, and five years later were making vital contributions to the Japanese in the aftermath of the disastrous earthquake of 1923.

The White epic is a continuing one, built on the solid foundations of the past. Thomas White, who died in 1914, left a legacy he little envisioned!

White Motor Corporation

(Top) Canadian troops were transported and supplied during World War I by White trucks. (Bottom) In 1912 Czar Nicholas of Russia witnessed competitive truck tests and, as a result, the Russian War Department ordered ten 3-ton Whites. At that time, it was the largest foreign order for American trucks ever delivered. Later the Russian government operated more than 4,000 White trucks in its war effort. This photo shows the czar inspecting his White Squadron at St. Petersburg.

Hard-tired Whites with canvas-topped cabs delivered gasoline for the Union Oil Company of California. In 1918, partly because of war-time successes, White discontinued making automobiles to concentrate on trucks like these.

Union Oil Company of California

Union Oil Company of California

The classic lines of the Packard radiator became almost as well recognized as the motor bonnet of the "Bulldog" Mack. It marked trucks and automobiles alike. Packard motor vehicles dated back to 1899 when James Ward Packard completed and ran his first single-cylinder model in Warren, Ohio, six years after he had drawn the plans.

As HISTORY was to prove, for every winner there were at least 20 losers in the fiercely competitive truck manufacturing business. Some of those whose names ultimately disappeared enjoyed unusual success during their hey-day, only to succumb in later years. One of these was Packard.

In 1884 James Ward Packard emerged from Lehigh University with a degree in mechanical engineering. With his brother—William D.—he established the Packard Electric Company in Warren, Ohio, during the following year.

The cable manufacturing business was successful, but by the early 1890s, James Packard was swept up in the mounting enthusiasm for automotive transportation. In 1893 he already had his first car "on paper"—but the panic that year prevented further progress. Six years later he finally built a spindly one-cylinder, tiller-guided runabout which would ultimately make Packard's name a household word for more than half a century.

In the beginning, though, it was not so easy. The Packard brothers, with George L. Weiss of Cleveland, created the New York and Ohio Automobile Company, dropping the "New York" soon after. An early buyer was Henry Bourne Joy, to whom Henry Ford had refused to sell his unfinished auto. Joy was so pleased with his Packard that he went to Warren to discuss business with the brothers; he ended up as president of the company.

The firm's name was changed to the Packard Motor Car Company and moved to Detroit—but the creator of the product decided to remain in Warren, becoming chairman of the board in absentia while Joy assumed control of the business. That was in 1903, the same year in which Tom Fetch drove "Old Pacific," a one-cylinder Packard, from San Francisco to New York. Though it took him almost two months, the resultant publicity—plus the substantial capital Joy was able to bring into the company — established Packard as a solid operation. By 1905 the firm was also making trucks.

In the period before World War I, the three Ps—Packard, Peerless and Pierce-Arrow—were respected leaders in the field of quality automobiles. All three of them also produced outstanding commercial vehicles. In 1912 a Packard truck was the first to cross the continent from east to west, leaving New York City on July 8 and arriving in San Francisco on August 24. It carried a three-ton load all the way. The trip was widely hailed as another break-through for motor transportation, and it helped Packard truck sales at a time when many other firms were trying to get a foothold in the market.

During World War I the Packard company produced trucks, Liberty engines and other military necessities. In the post-war period, however, it bowed out of the truck field to concentrate on automobiles. Finally, in 1958, the name disappeared altogether, exactly 30 years after the death of James Ward Packard, the electrical fixtures manufacturer whose pioneer tinkering won for him a niche in automotive history.

Washington Natural Gas Company

Public utilities often led the way in replacing horses with trucks. Prior to World War I, both the Seattle Lighting Company and Seattle City Light (two different operations) turned to Packard for motor transport.

Seattle Post-Intelligencer Library

New Jersey State Highway Department

In the early decades of motoring, Model T Fords were everywhere. They were adapted, rebuilt, re-designed and sometimes used just as they came from the factory. Few vehicles of any kind have ever played such a versatile role. This makeshift station wagon carried young New Jersey roadbuilders on a tour of inspection.

Ford

IT IS UNLIKELY that the automotive industry will ever produce another car with the historical significance and longevity of Henry Ford's famed Model T.

The story of this ubiquitous vehicle has been told and re-told. Ugly and colorless as it was, the "Tin Lizzie" has always been a nostalgic favorite. More than 15 million of them came off the revolutionary Ford production lines during the 19 years in which this single model persisted.

Born as a low-priced passenger car in 1908, the Model T ultimately became one of the most versatile motor conveyances ever devised. Literally dozens of body styles—ranging from sports roadsters to box-like delivery trucks—were introduced. But until 1927—when the model was finally scrapped for financial reasons—the unmistakable characteristics of the tenacious T were ever present.

In a way the Model T was sort of a mechanical chameleon. Though it could not change itself of its own accord, the tiny Ford was owned by millions of imaginative Americans, all seemingly obsessed with a desire to re-make the standard car. Accessory companies prospered with such slogans as: "Doll up your Ford for a dollar," "Hassler shock absorbers make a Ford ride as smoothly as a sleigh," "Double the value of your Ford with an H-W 'Snappy-Sport' body," "Disguise your Ford with a LAWCO streamline hood."

Washington Natural Gas Company

Fords were often jerry-built to fit specific assignments. They turned up as portable generators, compressors, machine shops and tool sheds.

But undoubtedly the most unique conversions came in the commercial field. Because of its functional simplicity and physical agelessness, the Model T often served several years in its original passenger function—and then went on to a "second career" as a concrete batch truck, a cream can conveyor, a mobile saw-sharpener's rig, a self-propelled tool shed or a gaudied-up advertising gimmick. It was lengthened, shortened, raised and lowered. It was souped up, torn down and made over. Though its primary role was to haul people, it ultimately carted almost every movable commodity in America not too big or too heavy for its limited capacity. That's why no truck history could justifiably exclude the Model T!

Henry Ford was 45 years old when his most noteworthy creation first emerged from the Detroit factory in 1908. Son of a Michigan farmer, a machinist's apprentice at 16 and an expert watch repairman by the time he was 20, young Ford had a mania for motors. As a teen-ager he built his first steam engine. He worked for the Drydock Engine Works, the Westinghouse Company, the Eagle Iron Works and the Detroit Electric Company, which became the Edison Illuminating Company. Each stop brought new mechanical experiences, but little monetary reward, to the still unrecognized genius. Just when his thinking turned to motorized transport is a moot point, but by 1893—the same year the Duryeas publicly unveiled their first auto—Henry Ford, too, built a horseless carriage. Unimpressed, his employer at the electric company offered to increase his salary from $125 a month to $150 if he would just

Central Motor Freight Association of Illinois

Henry Ford, the man whose Tin Lizzies put America on wheels, is shown at the tiller of his first quadricycle built in 1896. A dozen years later the Model T appeared.

August Fruehauf began building trailers in 1914 at his Detroit blacksmith shop. The first one he completed was for this adapted Ford Model T.

Central Motor Freight Association of Illinois

U. S. Post Office Department

Ford light delivery wagons proved that small gas-operated trucks were effective for in-city hauling, an area of transportation which many critics insisted would always be dominated by horses or electric vehicles.

quit tinkering with gas engines at home and get some sleep.

But by now Ford had a goal—and ultimately he quit his job to devote full time to perfecting the tiny quadricycle he introduced to the world in 1896. From 1899 to 1902 he was chief engineer for the Detroit Automobile Company, a notable failure, as was his succeeding Henry Ford Automobile Company. It was during this period, though, that the slow-to-start industrialist learned about a factor which would change his life and make his fortune: Speed!

With a two-cylinder car of his own creation, he entered a ten-mile race in October of 1901 against Alexander Winton of Cleveland, widely recognized as the national track champion. Before a crowd estimated at from 7,500 to 10,000, Henry Ford won the historical duel by three-quarters of a mile. The resultant publicity amazed him—and then he wisely determined to take advantage of it.

He built his renowned tiller-guided racer, the "999," and employed Barney Oldfield, the Salt Lake City bike pedaler, to drive it. Oldfield and the strange speed contraption were a winning combination, and on the strength of their suc-

Historical Collection, Title Insurance and Trust Company, San Diego

Before the Model T was discontinued in 1927, it appeared in every imaginable kind of style, from touring cars to baggage wagons.

cesses, the Ford Motor Company was organized on June 16, 1903.

The rest is history.

Ford's early autos created little sensation. A somewhat expensive six-cylinder Model K was a virtual failure. Only his Model N—a four cylinder roadster he introduced in 1905 and sold for $500—enjoyed promising sales. From those experiences, Ford developed his empire-building philosophy: Produce, on an assembly line basis, a moderately priced auto for the masses. With that in mind, the Model T was born!

How Henry Ford beat the Selden patent, developed the $5-a-day minimum wage and otherwise became a legendary figure even before his death in 1947 are not appropriate subjects for this book. His omnipresent Model T is, however, as it turned up in every corner of the United States, to move people, poultry, peas or packages with equal mechanical aloofness. Without question, it deserves a special niche in any history of commercial vehicles.

Songs were written about it; it was spoofed and derided by comedians and drugstore dandies; it provided constant material for cartoonists. As an auto or a truck, no one liked the Model T—but the people.

Swift & Company

Swift & Company replaced a mule team with this 1½-ton Ford truck. Note that even in the mid-twenties the idea of a rear-view mirror had still not caught on.

No vehicle seemed to challenge the imagination of the tinkerers like the Model T Ford. It was converted into hundreds of odd uses, both practical and impractical. An especially ingenious re-design was this ski-mobile.

Michigan State Highway Department

Fortune Transfer Company, Seattle, Washington

A teamster with high buttoned shoes wrestled this ancient Universal over the streets of Seattle before World War I. Even a heavy dew would cause the slick hard tires to spin and slide, but somehow the pioneer truckers managed to overcome the unusual problems which faced them in an era when motorized transport was still proving itself.

. . . and There Were Scores More!

Automotive hobbyists will be following the trails of pioneer trucks and cars for generations to come—and still the research will be far from complete.

All of a sudden, just before the turn of the century, everyone with four extra bicycle wheels wanted to attach a motor to them. The results ranged from dismal failure to the notable successes of Ransom E. Olds, Henry Ford, James Ward Packard, David Dunbar Buick, and, of course, the Duryea brothers. While the majority of the backshop inventors were obsessed with the desire to transport people, others were working just as diligently to produce motorized wagons which would be able to move goods more rapidly, more efficiently and more economically than man's faithful but obsolete friend, the horse.

The success stories are easy to chronicle. In many cases their histories are recorded, and models of the first vehicles have been located, restored and displayed prominently in museums and company showrooms. But the failures and the near-misses are something else again.

Who knows how many early-day trucks never got beyond the experimental model? How many hopeful builders struggled to complete self-powered delivery wagons which would revolutionize the world of commerce? Many never got out of the barn or the woodshed. Others sputtered feebly along the side streets and were ultimately abandoned. Some actually made it to market, where the vagaries of high finance and the stern test of competition finally did them in—after six months, a year or a decade.

This book, of course, is not meant to be an all-encompassing history. Its purpose is to recreate some of the atmosphere of the earliest years—and to set the historical sleuths to the task of rounding up the bits and pieces of an endless story. Acorn, Blaisdell, Cantono, Delia, Juno, Le Moon and Old Reliable were trucks of another age. How many others have been totally forgotten?

The Starters Were Many, The Survivors Few

BEFORE 1925 a long parade of new trucks chugged over the highways of history. A few of the names still exist. A few others were once prominent enough that they stir recollection. The majority, though, are totally unfamiliar to the present generation. The roll call of pioneer trucks contains steam, gas, distillate and electric models, strange three-wheelers and crude behemoths. Each represents a saga of hope, hard work and great personal involvement. Most of the names are like battlefield monuments to fallen soldiers. They had their brief day of glory—and are no longer remembered. America's pioneer trucks included the following:

A.
Ace
Acorn
Ahrens-Fox
Alco
American
American-LaFrance
American Napier
American Steamer
Anderson
Atlas
Atterbury
Auglaize
Auto Fore Carriage
Auto Wagon
(International)
Autocar
Available
Avery

B.
Baker Electric
Baldwin
Best
Bessemer
Biederman
Blaisdell
Blair
Bowling Green
Brasie
Broc Electric
Brockway
Brodesser
Brunner
Brush
Buckeye
Buick

C.
Cadillac
Cantono
Cartercar
Caterpillar
Chase
Chevrolet
Chicago Pneumatic
Cletrac
Cleveland
Clydesdale
Coleman
Colt
Columbia Electric
Commerce
Commercial
Steamer
Condor
Consolidated
Continental
Coppock
Corbitt
Couple-Gear
C. P. Truck
Crestmobile
C-T Electric
Curtis

D.
Daimler
Dart
Day-Elder
Delia
DeMotte
Denby
Denneed
Diamond T
Dickson Steamer
Doane
Dodge
Dorris
Duplex
Durant-Dort
Duryea

E.
Eisenbuth Horseless
Eldridge
Electric Vehicle
Electruck
Elk
Elwell-Parker
Empire State
Enkel
Esco

F.
Fageol
Famous
Federal
Federal Knight
Fischer
Fisher
Flanders
Flxible
Ford
Four Wheel Drive
Franklin
Frayer-Miller
Fulton

G.
Gabriel
Gaeth
Garford
Gary
General
General Electric
General Vehicle

The Republic Truck Company was once the largest exclusive manufacturer of trucks in the world. Though this model was of intense interest to the Dapper Dans of 1918, the Republic name was to disappear with the majority of its contemporaries, as new makes came and went like snowflakes on a hot rock.

Historical Collection, Title Insurance and Trust Company, San Diego

Historical Collection, Title Insurance and Trust Company, San Diego

In the post-war struggle for survival, many trucks took on similar appearances and often they were comparable in terms of capability. Consequently, the failure of one and the success of another was due in a large measure to advertising, salesmanship and business management rather than a truck's features, good or bad. Federals, as an example, were considered to be highly efficient units, but the name disappeared nonetheless.

Geneva
Gerlinger
Gersix
Giant
GMC
Goodyear
  (Experimental)
Gotfredson
Grabowsky
Graham
Gramm
Gramm-Bernstein
Grand
Grant
Grout
Guilder

H.
Hahn
Hanger
Hannah
Hart-Kraft
Harwood-Barley
Haynes-Apperson
Hendrickson
Herschmann
Hewitt
Hewitt & Lindstrom
Hoover
Howe
H.R.L. Truck
Hug
Hulbert
Hupp
Hurryton

I.
Indiana
International
  Electric
IHC (International
  Harvester)

J.
Jackson & Church
Jarrett
Jarvis
Jeffery
Juno

K.
Kansas City
  Commercial Car
Kato
Kavan
Kelly-Springfield
Kenworth
Kiblinger
Kimball
Kissel
Kleiber
Knox
Koehler
Krebs

L.
Lambert
Lange
Lansden
Le Moon
Liberty
Lincoln
Little Giant
Locomobile
Locomobile-Riker
Logan
Luitweiler
Luverne

M.
Maccarr
MacDonald
Mack
Mais
Marwin
Mason
Master
Maxim
Maxwell
Maxwell-Briscoe
McIntyre
Meiselbach
Menominee
Messinger
Metropolitan
Mitchell
Mobile Steamer
Mogul
Monitor
Moore
Mora
Moreland
Morgan
Morton Tractor
Motor Truck

N.
Nash Quad
National
Netco
Nevada
New England
New York
New York
  Auto-Truck
  (Compressed Air)
Noble
Nordyke & Marmon
North Western
Northwey
Nott

O.
Oakland
O. B. Truck
Ogden
O. K. Truck
Old Reliable

Oldsmobile (Olds)
Oliver
Oneida
Oshkosh
Overland

P.
Packard
Panhard
Paxon
Peerless
Pendell
People's
Perego-Clarkston
Peter Pirsch
Phelps Tractor
Phoenix
Pierce-Arrow
Piggins
Plymouth
Pope
Pope-Hartford
Pope Waverley
Poyer
Premier

R.
Randolph
Rainier
Rapid
Rauch & Lang
Reading
Rehberger
Relay
Reliance
Reo
Reo Democrat Wagon
Republic
Rigs-That-Run
Riker Electric
Robinson
Rockliff
Rowe
Rugby
Ruggles

S.
Sampson
Sandow
Sanford
Saurer
Sayers & Scovill
Schacht
Seagrave
Selden
Service
Signal
Six-Wheel
Standard
Stanley
Star
Star-Flee
Stegeman
Steinmetz
Sterling
Sternberg
Steward
Stewart
Studebaker
Sturgis
Stutz
Sullivan
Super

T.
Temple
Thomas
Titan
Torbensen
Traffic
Transport
Triple

U.
Union
United
United States
Universal

V.
Veale
Velie
Vim
Vulcan

W.
Wachusett
Walker
Walter
Ward
Washington
Waterous
Waverley Electric
Webb
Werner
White
Wichita
Wilcox
Will
Wilson
Wing Work Wagon
Winther
Winton
Wisconsin
Wolverine
Wonder
Woods Electric
World
Worth

Y.
Yellow Truck

Frank R. and William B. Fageol reputedly built the first gas-operated car in Iowa in 1899, after which they moved to California to open an automobile sales agency. They ended up as successful truck manufacturers, though they twice shifted their operations between the West Coast and Ohio before they sold out to the American Car and Foundry Company in 1925. They had originally hoped to build a $12,000 super-car, but World War I thwarted them.

Harrah's Automobile Collection, Reno, Nevada

LeTourneau-Westinghouse Company

An enclosed chain drive was a feature of this Avery truck manufactured in Peoria, Illinois. The company dated back to 1869 when Robert H. and C. M. Avery began to make and sell farm machinery. The firm had an international market by the time it entered the truck manufacturing business just prior to World War I.

Sagas of Success — and Failure

EVERY ATTEMPT to make and market a motor truck had its own unique story. There were hundreds of such tales of hardship and hope as the visionaries of the past contributed their individual efforts—sometimes feeble, sometimes far-reaching—to the ultimate product of the future.

Unfortunately, the great majority of these ambitious dreams ended in dismal failure for one or more of countless reasons. Many of the men who tried to build revolutionary vehicles were extremely limited in ability, and their fond reveries were unable to overcome their mechanical deficiencies. There were others who were capable of producing trucks of considerable promise, but financial shortcomings and legal snarls prevented them from getting beyond the fringes of success.

Some of the stories were quite unusual.

In 1858 Major General Joseph R. Brown, an

A Crestmobile delivery van.

Historical Collection, Title Insurance and Trust Company, San Diego

The Autocar Company grew out of the Pittsburgh Motor Vehicle Company founded in 1898 by Louis S. Clarke and two brothers. The firm was re-named when it was moved to Ardmore, Pennsylvania, in 1900. It produced shaft-driven automobiles before it turned to trucks later in the decade. Ultimately Autocar became a subsidiary of the White Motor Corporation.

Pennsylvania Historical and Museum Commission, Harrisburg

As competition got keener, manufacturing processes had to be improved. Henry Ford's assembly line techniques could not always be adapted to truck production, however, because of smaller quantities and special features required by the market. Workers here were spray-painting new Autocar trucks at the Ardmore, Pennsylvania, plant in 1923.

Indian agent in Minnesota, conceived the idea of a self-propelled road vehicle to deliver supplies to the frontier territories. Four years later an enormous steam traction engine—designed for the ambitious purpose—was completed by John A. Reed of New York City and tested on the streets of that burgeoning metropolis. Then, by rail and river steamer, it was transported all the way to Nebraska City, an important staging point for westward migration. The Reed-mobile arrived aboard the Steamer *West Wind* on July 12, 1862, and was appropriately welcomed with typical frontier frenzy and excitement. A string of wagons was attached to the rear of the giant vehicle, and scores of delighted people were towed up and down the earthen streets of the bustling village on the Missouri River.

For ten days the cumbersome "truck" remained in Nebraska City as preparations were completed for its maiden trip to Denver. Finally, on July 22, 1862, the giant machine clanked out of town, amid the hooray-and-hoopla such a revolutionary event demanded.

History, sadly enough, records that Reed's en-

George A. Brockway's first truck in 1912 was an unpretentious narrow-wheeled horse-cart with motor. Observers gave it little chance of success in competition with more sophisticated trucks already in existence. But the Brockway Motor Company kept improving its product, and by the early 1920s was producing substantial vehicles.

Brockway Motor Trucks

Brockway Motor Trucks

Truck and Coach Division, General Motors Corporation

The original Cartercar was built in the Michigan State Prison where its designer, Byron T. Carter, was superintendent of the machine shop. In 1910 the Cartercar Company was one of many bought up by William Crapo Durant and his original General Motors Company. Included in the Cartercar line was this delivery truck.

gine never made it! Seven miles from its starting point, the steamer broke down and had to be abandoned. For a time, J. Sterling Morton, a frontier newspaperman and tub-thumper for Nebraska, stored the mechanical derelict—but with the detractions of the Civil War and the coming of the railroad, the machine was almost forgotten. Eventually it was sold for $200 and used to operate a mill. Thus ended a noble experiment in motorized transport which was four decades ahead of its time.

Reed's vehicle could hardly be called a truck in the modern sense of the word, but General Brown's concept of hauling merchandise from one city to another by self-powered conveyances over roadways and not rails was certainly a valiant attempt to develop a "trucking" operation.

No doubt there were many isolated schemes and dreams to create a self-powered land wagon of some sort, but there was little noteworthy achievement until the horseless carriage era

Lansing Division, White Motor Corporation

Diamond T has been a respected name in the automotive industry since 1905 when C. A. Tilt marketed his first passenger car. In 1911 he produced a truck ordered by a customer and thereafter concentrated on commercial vehicles only. The Diamond T Motor Truck Company became a wholly-owned subsidiary of the White Motor Corporation in 1958.

Dodge Public Relations

This rebuilt Dodge pickup truck dates back to 1917; the flapper is part of a later-day promotion. Horace and John Dodge unveiled their first auto—"Old Betsy"—on November 14, 1914, though they had been making parts and motors for Ford and other manufacturers since 1901. Dodge ambulances, command cars and troop carriers were ever-present during World War I, and after the armistice, became the basis of the company's truck line.

dawned abruptly in the 1890s. Then, seemingly, the pent-up desires of centuries erupted in a great flurry of activity. While the majority of inventors and manufacturers were caught up in the excitement of producing pleasure cars, there were also those who visualized the new vehicles in important commercial roles.

In Chicago Charles E. Woods, an electrical engineer and successful carriage builder, pondered the situation at length, finally concluding that small delivery vans would be the first practical business application of self-propelled vehicles. Well before the turn of the century, Woods had his firm producing what some historians consider to be the first motor wagons manufactured in quantity for commercial use. These tiny trucks were powered by two 1200-watt electric motors capable of operating for five hours on a 32-cell battery. They were steered by a vertical rod on the left side fitted with a streetcar brake handle.

But Woods was not alone!

In 1896 A. L. Riker, a New York attorney turned mechanic, built a four-wheeled electric car simply by bolting two bicycles together and adding a power unit. Two years later he had an electric delivery wagon on display in Madison Square Garden. That same year—1898—the American Electric Vehicle Company unveiled its first commercial Waverley in Indianapolis.

Meanwhile, the exponents of gas-operated vehicles were moving in the same direction. Alexander Winton had eight gas commercial vans under production in October of 1898; they were merely panel bodies mounted on the regular

Even in the early days trucks were designed for specific purposes. "Low-boys" of several makes—like this California-built Doane—were introduced for dock-side transportation, the moving-and-storage industry, the hauling of newsprint and other heavy cargoes. This picture was taken in Fresno, California, 1921.

Western Trucking Magazine

GMC's "Big Brute" was a far cry from the original Grabowsky. In the early 1920s, power and performance became key promotion characteristics as truck manufacturers competed against one another instead of their old "enemy," the horse. Before 1916 few trucks could have climbed this ramp with a full load.

Truck and Coach Division, General Motors Corporation

Winton pleasure chassis. Concurrently, the Duryeas in Springfield, Massachusetts, were likewise converting a three-wheel passenger car for delivery assignments. The Pope Manufacturing Company of Hartford, Connecticut, also came on the market with a similar motorized tricycle.

At this point in history, the genealogy of motor trucks becomes an almost hopeless hodgepodge, with the emergence of new companies, the conversion of bicycle plants and the never-ending financial re-alignments of existing firms. Meanwhile, there were the scores of individual efforts adding to the confusion from one end of the country to the other.

In San Leandro, California, the Best Manufacturing Company tried to revive the concept of the

Nugent's Transfer & Storage Company, Miles City, Montana

Prominent among the pioneer truck makes was the Garford. Like so many others, it dropped out of existence in spite of its wide popularity before and after World War I.

Historical Collection, Title Insurance and Trust Company, San Diego

In the highly competitive period after World War I, scores of body styles were made available by truck manufacturers. This custom van was mounted on a Federal chassis.

The Gersix—later Kenworth—was one of the few trucks manufactured in the Pacific Northwest.

Kenworth Motor Truck Company

There was a Hoover truck long before there was a U. S. President of that name. This was the 1917 model of the short-lived vehicle.

U. S. Post Office Department

ill-fated Reed steam tractor of 1862. Its gargantuan internal combustion machine was designed, hopefully, to tow a pair of trailers carrying a total of 60 tons of merchandise. The technology of 1898, however, was not quite up to such ambitious goals, though several Best machines of that vintage found some success in farm work.

In Chicago an uninhibited inventor proposed another commercial use for self-propelled contrivances. His design for an "autogoat" consisted of an electric vehicle with an ingenious (though impractical) system of mechanical arms which reached out and picked up debris from the streets and gutters. Needless to say, not every idea was a brilliant one!

The "legitimate" truck, as it finally evolved,

This unusual bus was an experimental model built by Goodyear to demonstrate the practicability of tandem rear wheels. In the early 1920s, the company also utilized trucks of its own design to promote new tire concepts. When manufacturers were convinced that six smaller tires were better than four big ones, the tests were discontinued.

The Goodyear Tire & Rubber Company

(Top) Jerrold B. Winther

(Bottom) Standard Oil Company of California

(Top) Thomas B. Jeffery, a bicycle manufacturer, turned to automobiles after the turn of the century and introduced the G & J car. Soon after, the name was changed to Rambler, his bike trademark. In the truck field the Jeffery Company of Kenosha, Wisconsin, developed a successful four-wheel-drive model which ultimately became the Nash Quad. Lesser known was this Jeffery pickup, the first vehicle the company equipped with pneumatic tires. (Bottom) Kleiber trucks had a relatively short history. Note the handy chock block behind the rear wheel.

Kelly-Springfield Tire Company

The Kelly-Springfield name stood for tires, trucks and heavy road equipment, all evident in this early photo. The easily recognizable snub-nosed Kellys were popular in the pre-World War I era, but they failed to survive the competitive aftermath.

came into being after 1900. While electrics and steamers were to hold on for ten years or more, gas vehicles rapidly took the lead, although no early manufacturers gave any indication that they would run away with the market. As a matter of fact, of the ten American companies which proposed to enter the first commercial car contest in 1903 (see Page 36), not one of them lasted out the decade as a builder of trucks. By then the Mack brothers had a number of vehicles in use; White steamers of several sizes had been

The Moreland truck on the left featured an interesting innovation. Holes were drilled through the solid rubber tires on the theory that this would provide more "give" and thus a smoother ride. Success was limited.

Historical Collection, Title Insurance and Trust Company, San Diego

sold; Max Grabowsky had introduced his power wagon, and the first Studebaker electrics were on the market.

The emphasis was on passenger autos, but many manufacturers of pleasure cars popped in and out of the commercial field, thus complicating the chronology of the motor truck story. Almost all of the early truck builders had first produced passenger vehicles or continued to make them along with their commercial line.

George N. Pierce, a bicycle and bird cage manufacturer, had been making cars for ten years before he introduced the first Pierce-Arrow truck. The original Diamond T was an auto built by C. A. Tilt in 1905; the first truck to bear the name came out in 1911. The initial Packard runabout of 1899 preceded the first Packard truck by five years. The Peerless Manufacturing Company of Cleveland (which had originally been established in Cincinnati in 1869 to make clothes wringers) became the Peerless Motor Car Company with the advent of its tiny three-wheeled motorette at the turn of the century. Its highly respected heavy trucks came later. Louis S. Clarke with two brothers founded the Pittsburgh Motor Vehicle Company in 1898 to manufacture one of the earliest shaft-driven autos. Two years later the firm moved to Ardmore, Pennsylvania, changed its name to the Autocar Company and continued to make passenger vehicles for seven years before it started to produce the trucks which ultimately made it famous. The first FWD was a power-packed auto called the "Battleship." Preceding the Jeffery Quad was the popular Rambler. Even the mighty Mack descended from

Michigan State Highway Department

When Charles W. Nash bought the Thomas B. Jeffery Company in 1916, one of the chief assets was the firm's four-wheel-drive truck which became famous in World War I as the Nash Quad. This war-surplus model was equipped with road-grading gear.

Prior to World War I, Packard—with Peerless and Pierce-Arrow—constituted the 3 Ps, noted for fine passenger cars. The trio also produced popular trucks like this pair of Packards owned by Armour and Company.

Harrah's Automobile Collection, Reno, Nevada

(Top) Harrah's Automobile Collection, Reno, Nevada

(Bottom) Truck and Coach Division, General Motors Corporation

(Top) In 1901 the George N. Pierce Company of Buffalo, New York, introduced the famed Pierce-Arrow automobiles. Before the end of the decade, the firm was also a leading manufacturer of trucks like this rugged worm-drive model.

(Bottom) A Rapid seat-over-engine truck demonstrated its power by towing a load of telephone poles on a crude wagon-wheel trailer, circa 1910. The Rapid was one of the predecessors of the GMC truck.

a bus! But the purpose of this book is not to stack detail upon detail, but rather to present a broad-brush sketch of a new industry as it alternately limped, leaped and occasionally languished through its adolescent years. The total lack of precedent—added to the fact that developments came so rapidly that they were almost impossible to assimilate—kept the pioneer truck builders

(Top) U S. Bureau of Public Roads Photo in The National Archives

(Bottom) Standard Oil Company of California

(Top) A five-ton Sampson forded a stream near Leeds, Missouri, in the spring of 1912. Later that year another truck made by the Alden Sampson Manufacturing Company of Detroit failed in the U. S. Army's gruelling road test from Washington, D. C., to Fort Benjamin Harrison, Indiana. Like many contemporaries, the Sampson ultimately disappeared. (Bottom) A Moreland distillate truck leaving Los Angeles on a speed run in 1913.

stumbling down their own individual trails, hoping that their ideas of design would survive the scramble for acceptance.

In the period from 1900 to 1910 the problem was not necessarily to produce the best truck in the world, but to produce *any* kind of a truck at all! It was 1907 before a thousand of them were produced in any one year. Because of the concentration of manufacturing centers, most of the nation was yet to see a factory-made model by the end of 1910 when fewer than 15,000 commercial vehicles existed.

In the light of this development, it is easy to understand the catalystic role played by World War I. It separated the "dogs" from the producers. It made truck production a big business rather than a hit-or-miss proposition into which almost any self-styled mechanic could wander without previous experience. The failure rate was exceedingly high, but it was a circumstance in which the victim could get up, dust himself off and hire out to a survivor. Out of such an unsteady, disorganized beginning, a giant industry emerged.

Swift & Company

Like most trucks of its day, this Packard featured a cab which was open and airy. By this time (circa 1920) Packard had abandoned the chain drive and shifted the steering column to the lefthand side.

American Trucking Associations, Inc.

This 1911 White was open to the elements. Being a truck driver was a good job—when the weather was ideal. But when the winds blew and snow fell, pioneer teamsters had to be a hardy lot.

The Winther Motor Truck Company was established in Kenosha, Wisconsin, in 1916 following the purchase of the Thomas B. Jeffery Company by Nash. Martin P. Winther, an engineer for Jeffery, started his own firm rather than join the new organization. Winther built a good truck (above), but his company didn't survive the post-war decline.

Jerrold B. Winther

Chew Sing
FRESH FRUIT & VEGETABLES

(Opposite page) Harrah's Automobile Collection, Reno, Nevada

FWD Corporation

Farm work was Old Dobbin's final domain—and in time the motor truck invaded that arena, too. This three-ton Four Wheel Drive hauling a heavy load of beans from a California field proved the capabilities of work trucks operating on plowed ground. The battlefields of France had not stopped them; why should a flat, dry garden?

Beans, Bread, Beer and Butter

MOTOR TRUCKS HELPED CHANGE the eating habits of America!

The movement of perishables—dairy products, meat, fish, fruit, vegetables and bakery goods—had been extremely limited before 1900. Railroads could make the long haul satisfactorily and horses were capable of in-city deliveries, albeit ploddingly. Meanwhile, the intermediate runs—between towns, between states and from farm-to-market—were severely neglected.

Only the farmers close to the cities could deliver sweet cream by horse and wagon. Fresh milk supplies depended upon how fast Old Dobbin could clippity-clop into town. It was an era of smoked sausages, cured hams and corned beef . . . when cheeses and sauerkraut and pickled pigs feet would last, but fresh meat, fresh vegetables and fresh milk had to be consumed within a few short miles of their source—or not at all.

Persistence may have won the race for the turtle, but it took speed to deliver fresh eggs, unspoiled oysters and ripe tomatoes — especially when refrigeration was crude or non-existent.

Thus it was that the pioneer commercial vehi-

Truck and Coach Division, General Motors Corporation

(Opposite page) Fruit peddlers, rag pickers, milkmen, bakers and probably even candlestick makers adapted the Ford Model T to their particular needs. (Right) the delivery of foodstuffs was an important part of the trucking industry right from the beginning. This four-cylinder Rapid hauled ginger ale and other grocery products in Detroit, circa 1910.

Harrah's Automobile Collection, Reno, Nevada

The Coca-Cola drinkers of another generation were served by pioneer trucks across the nation. The truck on the right sported a rear-view mirror, a rare safety precaution for the early 1920s. The klaxon horn had replaced the squeeze bulb and windshields were becoming more common, but truck manufacturers still had a long way to go.

cles putt-putted into a great void. Even the earliest trucks were able to triple and quadruple the speed of delivery. More than that, they carried greater loads and added considerably to the daily range of service. While a horse and wagon could only go 20 miles in a working day, a truck could make 80. What's more the truck could do it every day—and with the coming of the first feeble headlights, it could work around the clock, too.

While the railroads were able to make good time once under way, they still had to depend upon the horse to get the shipment to the railhead and then to move it from the depot to the customer. The delays enroute meant that only the hardiest of foodstuffs could survive the trip.

So the motor vehicle found ready acceptance—once it proved that it could improve a very bad situation. Cudahy, Armour, Swift, Heinz, Amer-

Meat packers, ever anxious to speed up the movement of their products before refrigeration was widely used, turned to motor trucks to solve their problem. This Packard with body enclosed was a much more sanitary and efficient way to haul beef halves than in open horse-drawn wagons with a tarp or a few gunny sacks for covering.

Automobile Manufacturers Association, Inc.

Washington State Department of Highways

Corn starch, shredded wheat and chewing tobacco were included in the load of this vintage pickup truck. With hard tires on the rear of his vehicle, the driver had to control his speed and watch his route or the odds against retaining his cargo were formidable. But proud, indeed, were the young men who got to drive a truck in those days.

ican Tea and dozens of other alert food suppliers began to replace teams with trucks. They discovered, too, that gas-operated machines did not attract flies like the time-honored hay-burners—and that fact automatically contributed to improved health standards in food-handling.

There was another point to consider.

Thomas Edison insisted that the horse was the least efficient motor ever built, and he had statistics to prove his point. To deliver a meager thermal efficiency output of two per cent, a horse ate something like 12,000 pounds of food a year.

This box-like Chevrolet panel truck of the early twenties featured an adjustable windshield. The driver sat almost midway back on the frame. The door on his side of the vehicle was worthless in terms of accessibility, but at long last an effort was being made to give the buffetted teamsters some protection from the weather.

Chevrolet Division, General Motors Corporation

Fruehauf Corporation

August Fruehauf and Otto Neumann, whom Fruehauf hired as a blacksmith in 1911, were pioneer trailer builders who helped add a new dimension to trucking. This "Bulldog" Mack increased its load two-fold with a Fruehauf rig.

He ate on Sundays and holidays and on the days he was resting. He nibbled when he was ill or lame. He was at the oat box or hay manger in winter whether he was snowed in or not. A motor truck, Edison preached, only used fuel when it was on the job.

In 1911—when the truck was rapidly emerging from its embryonic stage—the National Bureau of Agriculture reported that there were 17,344,000 horses and 3,754,000 mules in the United States. Just to produce the 73,000,000 tons of hay they ate annually would have taken a farm as large as the combined states of Iowa, Indiana, Illinois and Ohio. Needless to say, America was devoting millions of valuable acres to the raising of food for work animals and not for people.

Good roads, of course, were part and parcel of the story. Without them a mired truck would have been no better than a hand-cart. So it was really a combination of the motor vehicle and greatly improving farm-to-market byways which brought new dimensions to the American dinner table. Whether or not any great effort would have been made to build the roads had the horseless carriage not materialized is another question.

The sudden availability of a growing number of trucks—in all fields of commerce—did not necessarily result in immediate and wholesale conversion to this new form of transportation, however. It did little good to have a vehicle capable of rushing fresh produce, newly churned butter or live chickens into a metropolitan market from a farm community two counties away if the farmers were skeptics and wouldn't cooperate on the timing involved. What facilities existed were geared to horses. There were no service stations along the way. Truck owners and drivers were inexperienced, not only in terms of handling their vehicles, but in knowing what they were capable of accomplishing.

Truck owners were proud of their vehicles when motor transport was still relatively new. They never missed an opportunity to include them in local festivities, a fact which was not particularly appreciated by horse-owners. In 1914 Charles S. Hardy's Bay City Market displayed his "fleet" in a San Diego parade.

Historical Collection, Title Insurance and Trust Company, San Diego

FWD Corporation

Motorized transportation gave agricultural production a healthy boost, directly and indirectly. It permitted farmers to move more of their products faster and farther. It placed new emphasis on the farm-to-market roads which were developed as trucks and autos began to venture out of the cities and towns.

What was needed was a gigantic educational program—but at the time there was no organized industry to do the job, and, consequently, the result was a nation-wide learn-as-you-go adventure, liberally sprinkled with disconcerting failures and stuttering successes. Henry Ford reputedly said: "The trouble with the school of experience is that the graduates are too old to go to work." Unfortunately, that was the only school available to the pioneers of motor transportation; there was nothing to do but plunge!

Teamsters whose only previous experience was with horses suddenly found themselves at the steering wheels of impersonal motorized monsters about which they knew very little. Many who drove electrics had to learn the hard way how to plan their routes so they'd make it back to the "barn" before they were juiceless. Pilots of vintage steamers had to be coal stokers and automotive plumbers to keep fires hot and coil pipes from leaking. Some of the first gas trucks were more temperamental than a high-spirited team, but by trial and error, drivers soon learned to cope with the mechanical eccentricities of their new steeds.

In the early days, more than one dairy hauler, for instance, over-estimated the power of his truck on a hill and had to take remedial action. It usually consisted of unloading half of the heavy, brim-full cream cans at the foot of the incline, driving to the top with the rest, unloading that half, returning for the remainder—and then re-loading everything before chugging up the road again. Sometimes this process had to be repeated two or three times before the end of the route.

U. S. Department of Agriculture

In the summer of 1851 several tons of butter were shipped from Ogdensburg, New York, to Boston in a wooden railroad boxcar which had been insulated with sawdust and packed with ice. This was reputedly the first long-distance refrigerated hauling of such a perishable item. The techniques of refrigeration improved very little during the next half century, and when the first trucks came along, they concentrated on short-run deliveries where icing was seldom needed. By the twenties, however, bigger and better vehicles were making longer hauls, and the need for refrigerated units was vital to the future of the industry. As usual, necessity spurred the required inventions.

Obviously, truck-driving in the hard-tire era required muscle and stamina—along with the innate intelligence and manual dexterity necessary to master a cantankerous Hewitt, a recalcitrant Avery or a stubborn Sampson.

But pioneers (of any kind) have never had it easy, and it is difficult for the more sophisticated inhabitants of a later generation to visualize the

This load of melons in a vintage International Harvester Auto Wagon is symbolic of the change which motor vehicles brought to farming. "Truck gardens" could be farther from market when the plodding horse was replaced. The concern about spoilage was reduced by every improvement which cut the time-lag between harvest and consumer.

The change-over, of course, was not immediate. By farm standards, the new-fangled contraptions were quite expensive. Farmers could raise hay and oats, but they had to buy gasoline and oil. Roads —even the ones called "highways" —were often just a series of chuckholes connected by muddy ruts. What's more, many farmers were just plain skeptical!

So truck ownership, in the beginning, was confined largely to town haulers who drove into the country to pick up cream cans, egg cases, poultry crates and fresh vegetables. Herding of cattle to stockyards and railroads continued for years, but as trucks and trailers got bigger and better, livestock, too, went to slaughter on hard rubber.

(Above and bottom right) U. S. Department of Agriculture

(Top) Fraser Valley Milk Producers Association, Burnaby, B. C.

The clinking of cream cans on country roads was an overture heralding the beginning of America's modern dairy industry. Trucks of all kinds chugged between local creameries and pickup points, making it possible for more farmers to sell sweet cream and fresh milk to city markets. Left above is a Brockway; below is a Packard. The chain-drive Model T, top right, used a farm-wagon trailer to double its load in the Fraser Valley of British Columbia.

hardships and unending aggravations of those who led the way. This is certainly true of the trucking industry as changes came so rapidly, and those who were involved started virtually from a dead-stop.

And there was, of course, a certain amount of reluctance to drop the reins to the past. Some of the first horseless carriages boasted whip sockets as part of their accessories. One lady inventor wanted to put a motor inside a mechanical horse-on-wheels so that the new vehicle wouldn't be such a drastic change. Many truck owners kept a team or two around "just in case." It was a wonderful era—an historical proving ground—as the centuries-old techniques of transportation were abruptly outmoded.

Pennsylvania Historical and Museum Commission, Harrisburg

(Opposite Page) Jerrold B. Winther

Historical Collection, Title Insurance and Trust Company, San Diego

The trucking industry got its start in the light delivery field in large Eastern cities. Steamers, electrics and putt-putting gas models scooted around among the horse-drawn wagons, proving that a new era was dawning. Many makers of passenger autos also produced small panel trucks to serve the growing demands for delivery vehicles.

Trucks at Work: 1,001 Uses!

EARLY IN THE nineteenth century Gridley Bryant's Granite Railway in Quincy, Massachusetts, carried the stone used for the Bunker Hill monument in horse-drawn trams over its three miles of track. In 1830 the Baltimore & Ohio Railroad began to haul freight on its 13-mile line between Baltimore and Ellicott's Mill.

The dawn of the railroad era in the United States supplemented, but did not replace, the basic means of transporting goods: by animal power.

In the same period, the 363-mile Erie Canal was built, and on October 26, 1825, a barge—the *Seneca Chief*—was dispatched from Buffalo with a barrel of Lake Erie water to be dumped into the Atlantic Ocean at New York City. This event emphasized the importance of water-borne commerce to the young nation.

Meanwhile, near Lancaster, Pennsylvania, the Conestoga Wagon (named after the Indians of the area) was created. With a three-team capacity of five tons, it was a vital factor in the trade of the age. Also, it was the prototype of the so-called "prairie schooner" which played a dominant role in the opening of the western frontier.

In cities and villages, oxen and horses tugged against yoke and whiffletree as they carried farm produce to mills and markets. The Mormons of 1847 used handcarts to transport their earthly possessions from Nauvoo, Illinois, to the valley of the Great Salt Lake.

In a general sense, these historical occasions

Harrah's Automobile Collection, Reno, Nevada

(Opposite page) One of the earliest snowplows was this four-wheel-drive Winther built in Kenosha, Wisconsin. In the pioneer era of motor travel, winter driving was rarely attempted; cars were drained and put on blocks until springtime. However, as roads and vehicles improved, the driving year was gradually extended around the calendar. Note the vicious spikes on the wheels. (Right) This Pierce-Arrow pickup with canopy carried double spares in 1914.

(Above) Washington State Department of Highways

(Below) National Ready Mixed Concrete Association

In 1916 Stephan Stepanian applied for a patent on the ready-mixed concrete unit shown in the sketch at right. Known as a "self-discharging motorized transit mixer," the then-unique vehicle was a harbinger of things to come. The application, however, was refused. After World War I, though, Stepanian's concept became reality and a whole new industry was born. Ready mixed concrete trucks, like the pioneer model above, gradually replaced the batch trucks which in less than a single decade had been substituted for horses or on-the-spot mixing.

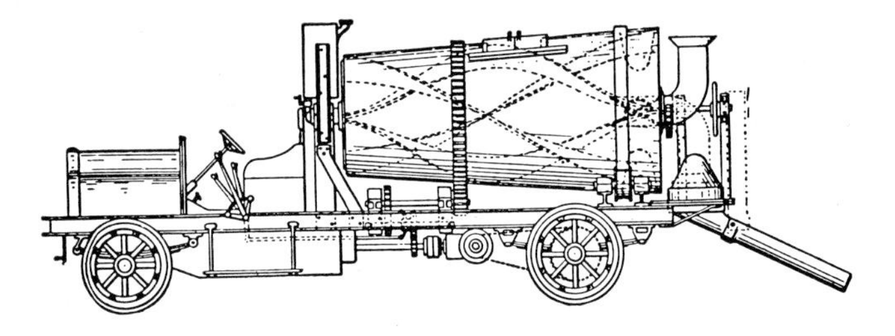

epitomized the methods of moving merchandise and materials in the United States when the first motor trucks appeared. Railroads were limited in scope by the same parallel strands of iron which otherwise made them so effective. Boats and barges, obviously, could travel only on the available waterways. Beyond a certain point in breeding, horses and oxen could be made no stronger or swifter—and little could be done to lessen the enormous amount of care and forage they demanded.

So it was that an unfilled transportation gap existed in the 1890s when the Automotive Age had its beginning. The crying need for greater efficiency, greater speed, greater pay-loads and more versatility of movement offered unlimited oppportunities for mechanic-inventors to develop a totally new approach to the shipment of goods. Whether they knew it at the time or not, the Whites, the Macks, the Stanleys and their fellow pioneers were on the threshold of a gigantic revolution.

The earliest trucks, as they emerged from blacksmith shops, carriage factories and bicycle plants bore little resemblance to the power wagons they ultimately became. Many of them looked like their horse-drawn counterparts — because

Pennsylvania Historical and Museum Commission, Harrisburg

A roller system on the truck bed permitted this teamster to unload a heavy stack of lumber by driving out from under it. Such were the innovations which gradually broadened the use of motorized transport.

Truck and Coach Division, General Motors Corporation

Block tires on the rear wheels gave this 3-ton Rapid the necessary traction to haul a heavy load of coal. It took plenty of muscle to manipulate trucks of this vintage with vertical steering posts and other relatively unrefined engineering principles. Note bashful Charlie mugging the camera over the left front wheel.

that's really what they were. People thought in terms of horses, and at first, manufacturers considered only a limited number of uses for self-propelled vans. If trucks could improve the in-city delivery situation, that would certainly be contribution enough.

But the vehicles themselves changed all that. Once on the job, they proved that they would be capable of endless tasks. All they needed were continuing increases in power and speed, the accessories to make night-time driving possible, adequate roads to travel on and owners imaginative enough to use them to full advantage. The key word, of course, was imagination!

Standard Oil Company of California

More autos and trucks meant greater demands for petroleum products. Motorized tankers, like this 1911 Peerless, were developed to meet the needs.

Seattle Transit System

(Top) Wherever construction work was done, trucks showed up in increasing numbers during the mid-twenties. By then horses were the exception. This photo shows a repair job on a street railway in Seattle, Washington.

(Below) Trucks were adapted to literally thousands of uses through ingenious devices such as this mobile platform for streetcar linemen. With no headlights, this vehicle had to return to the car barns before nightfall—but as a feeble precaution a kerosene lantern dangled from the rear.

Automobile Manufacturers Association, Inc.

We have already discussed in the previous chapter the role of trucks in the transportation of food products. In a similar manner they invaded a thousand-and-one other industries, modifying each of them in the process. Once businessmen stopped thinking "horse" and started thinking "truck," the scope of the latter increased immeasurably.

Gradually, additional uses of the truck's motor were developed. Automatic dump bodies and power winches — prosaic though they may seem — brought new versatility. There were special tank trucks, trucks mounted with snowplow gear and hole-drilling equipment. As early as 1916 the concept of the ready-mixed concrete carrier was advanced. The perfection of the four-wheel-drive system by the FWD and Jeffery companies made possible many off-the-road uses on farms, in the

This vintage International was made over into a mobile compressor and tool shed to permit railroad line crews to operate more efficiently. Incidentally, early-day Internationals and Kelly-Springfields looked much alike with their snub-nose motor bonnets.

Seattle Transit System

oil fields and for construction work. Truck designers created "low-boys" with their chassis hugging the earth, self-propelled cranes and derricks, armored vehicles for police work and money-hauling, livestock vans, water sprinklers and assorted reefers. A truck became many things to many users. Manufacturers began to think in terms of the job first, and then producing a vehicle to get the specific assignment accomplished. When this point occurred, the industry had "come of age!"

Until now, we have little considered the long-suffering teamsters who sat behind the tillers and steering wheels of the pioneer trucks. Without them the vehicles would have been worthless masses of machinery; there were times when the drivers would have preferred it that way.

Ben Rathjen, who operated a hard-tired monster on the washboard roads of South Dakota, reminisced: "There was one thing the old trucks had in common: they shook you so hard your ancestors felt it!"

Thousands of other drivers would no doubt echo a hearty "amen." Comfort was not an element of concern in the "good old days." Kidneys were expendable, and arms broken by backlashing motor cranks were considered a mere occupational hazard. Years went by before any real effort

Kelly-Springfield Tire Company

Before this truck-mounted automatic drill came along, it cost Pacific Telephone and Telegraph Company about three dollars apiece to dig post holes. The mechanical auger—driven by means of a universal shaft from the power take-off of this Caterpillar truck—permitted the phone company to cut its expenses to 31 cents per hole.

The Kahn-Wadsworth bill after World War I made possible the distribution of thousands of surplus military trucks to the 48 states for road-building purposes. The various highway departments received a conglomerate assortment of vehicles in the process, but local ingenuity adapted them to the needs of the particular area. This photo was taken in the shop area of the Oregon State Highway Department in Salem. The year was 1920.

Oregon State Highway Department

Nevada Department of Highways

After 1920 pneumatic tires became more and more popular. Manufacturers promoted the obvious improvements in driver comfort and the reduction in wear and tear on the vehicles themselves. Hard tires literally shook early-day trucks to pieces—not to mention what they did to the spines and kidneys of the pioneer teamsters. But pneumatic tires brought another set of problems. While the solid rubber "skins" wore down and occasionally "blew out" from excess friction, they were 100 per cent puncture-proof. The same couldn't be said for the pneumatics. That's why the Nevada Department of Highways fitted out the unusual magnet truck (above) to rid the state's roads of the steel villains which wreaked havoc on unsuspecting tires. A closeup of the magnet (below) shows how well it did its job.

Nevada Department of Highways

was made to perfect a decent windshield or to enclose truck cabs against the wind, the rain and the bitter cold.

"Sometimes we took the kerosene lamps, which we used for rear lights, and put them by our feet," recalled Vernon R. Fry of Carnation, Washington. "We had the choice of being asphyxiated by the fumes or freezing to death."

In the early days, some drivers had been with horses so long that when they got into emergency situations with trucks, they tried to stop them by

Truck-mounted pole rigs were included among the countless innovations which rapidly changed the role of the motor truck from a noble experiment to a commercial necessity.

American Trucking Associations, Inc.

(Above) Union Oil Company of California (Right) FWD Corporation

shouting "Whoa!" Others were so mechanically inept that they drove without oil, ground gears unmercifully and overloaded their vehicles till axles snapped and frames bent.

One of the few worthwhile by-products of World War I was the pool of experienced, well-trained drivers which the military services sent home from France and from the training camps on both sides of the ocean. On the Mexican border in 1916 the army had had to use civilian teamsters

The adaptation of trucks to the petroleum industry came quickly; after all, it was incongruous to use horses to supply the automotive industry. Tank trucks of all kinds were devised. "Old No. 28" (center right), an FWD, was a veteran of World War I before going to work in the oil fields. It was later featured in the movie, "Tulsa." The truck below is a Federal; the one at the right is a GMC.

(Below) Historical Collection, Title Insurance Company and Trust Company, San Diego. (Right) Truck and Coach Division, General Motors Corporation

Automobile Manufacturers Association, Inc.

Trucks were already in use by police departments before 1910. Motorized paddy wagons like these vintage Rapids gave the Indianapolis law officers unusual stature. The vehicles weren't much for speed—but then they seldom had to chase anything faster than a run-away team. Even policemen in those days didn't use rear-view mirrors.

because not enough men in uniform could handle trucks. Steps were taken immediately to correct this deficiency, and by Armistice Day thousands of doughboys had been schooled in mechanics and vehicle operation. These men had a greater appreciation for motors, and, in the post-war period, many of them found jobs driving the thousands of surplus trucks which were released for peace-time uses.

But being a truck driver in the pioneer period was not the world's greatest job!

While wages varied across the country and from time to time, pre-war teamsters often worked from dawn till dark for two dollars a day. This figure improved slightly in the early twenties, but conditions were ripe for union organization. Many drivers—especially in the big cities—were on a day-to-day basis. Each morning they would appear at the truck "barns" for a ritual called "shape-up." Owners would select as many drivers as were required, and the men who didn't get a truck would rush to the next garage or warehouse in hopes of landing a daily assignment. This arrangement was detrimental to all parties. Drivers were never sure of work, a factor which caused many potentially good men to seek other occupations. Owners often foolishly assigned

Dodge Public Relations

By 1925 commercial trucks represented 20 per cent of Dodge Brothers' production. This paddy wagon of that year was a considerable improvement over the ancient models above. The advent of Prohibition, however, made it necessary for police forces to modernize to keep even with the bootleggers of the era.

their expensive trucks and valuable cargoes to "fly-by-nighters" who—as one writer of the period put it—"they normally wouldn't have trusted to carry their wives' Sunday hats across the street."

Drivers not only piloted their trucks, but they loaded and unloaded, made mechanical repairs, changed tires at all-too-frequent intervals and often had to collect for the shipment. Sometimes they had to carry firearms when they had valuable cargoes like silk or cigarettes. Truck hi-jackers were a constant threat on certain runs.

Under the circumstances drivers sought solutions through organization.

In 1903—the year the Ford Motor Company was established—the Team Drivers' International Union and the National Teamsters of Chicago were merged to form the International Brotherhood of Teamsters. As early as 1850 the draymen of San Francisco had a local affiliation, but not until 1899 — under the leadership of Samuel Gompers—was the scope broadened and the Team Drivers' International organized.

The new amalgamated union floundered for several years until, in 1908, Daniel Joseph Tobin

U. S. Post Office Department

The U. S. Post Office Department first tested motorized equipment before the turn of the century. Various conveyances were tried, including this interesting three-wheeler which looked a little like a self-propelled coffin.

To protect valuable mail shipments, this GMC was fitted with a special armored cab. With pistol drawn, a plainclothes guard demonstrated that the U. S. Post Office Department meant business. The particular vehicle shown here operated in the nation's capital during the twenties.

Truck and Coach Division, General Motors Corporation

Pennsylvania Historical and Museum Commission, Harrisburg

In the brief span of years covered by this book, transportation on land and in the air made revolutionary advances. In less than three decades, the speed of mail deliveries in the United States was vastly improved. Horse-drawn equipment, like the carrier's buggy below, gave way to motorized tricycles, trucks and airplanes. The picture above was taken in Holyoke, Massachusetts, in the mid-twenties when air mail services were being widely adopted.

became its president. Born in Ireland, garrulous "Uncle Dan" came to the United States alone as a boy of 14. After a brief schooling, he took a job as a team driver in Boston at $11 for a 70-hour week. When he became head of the Teamsters, the union was debt-ridden and relatively ineffective. The emphasis was still on horses. Only 1,500 trucks were made in the year Tobin assumed the presidency; there was some concern about the threat of "automation," but mostly the 33-year-old union leader concentrated on the problems at hand.

By 1913 membership was up, there was money in the treasury and it was becoming quite obvious that trucks were not just a passing fancy. That year Dave Beck, who was to succeed Tobin in

U. S. Post Office Department

Pennsylvania Historical and Museum Commission, Harrisburg

Regular Common Carrier Conference

Automobile Manufacturers Association, Inc.

1952, was a teen-age laundry worker in Seattle, Washington. On February 14, 1913, another future union president—James Riddle Hoffa—was born to a coal miner and his wife in Brazil, Indiana. More than 23,000 trucks came off production lines, and Tobin's organization strengthened its jurisdictional claim "over all teamsters and helpers, chauffeurs and helpers, and men who are employed on horses, harness, carriages, or automobiles, in and around stables and garages."

From that point on, unionism became more and more of a factor in motor transportation as hard-tired trucks and hard-fisted labor representatives grew up together.

All of these things were part of the early history of trucks and trucking. There were the first "wild cat" operators who took hauling jobs wherever and whenever they could find them.

Motorized delivery service caught on rapidly in the major cities of the U. S. Leading department stores—like R. H. Macy (above), Saks, John Wanamaker and others—compared horses with trucks and promptly adopted the latter for economic reasons. Major express companies, which had maintained huge stables and footed gigantic feed bills, made the switch to self-propelled vehicles even before the trucks had totally proved themselves.

Automobile Manufacturers Association, Inc.

Automobile Manufacturers Association, Inc.

The air-cooled auto built by H. A. Knox in Springfield, Massachusetts, was an early favorite of horseless-carriage devotees. Trucks produced by the same manufacturer were similarly successful, virtually running away with the first commercial vehicle contest honors in 1903. Waterless Knoxes were hauled by truck from factory to sales agency, with appproriate banners announcing the fact. Unfortunately, the demise of the Knox was as rapid as its rise.

There were the ambitious one-truck outfits like Lee & Eastes in Washington State which started hauling yeast and then grew into a major transportation company. There were men like Earle Halliburton, who bought five surplus FWDs after World War I and parlayed an idea into a multimillion dollar oil well cementing business.

Prohibition involved trucks, too. Bootleggers used souped-up models for rum-running—or tried to get whiskey smuggled through police cordons in seemingly legitimate cargoes. Most truck owners, fearful of losing valuable franchises, withstood the temptation — but individual drivers, working for inadequate wages, occasionally gambled on sneaking by with illegal booze hidden in a load of furniture, hardware or groceries. If they were lucky, there was a payoff of ten dollars or more a case at the end of the line.

Any time there was something to haul, sooner or later a truck got into the act!

Trucking history is filled with thousands of stories of small companies which started with one or two vehicles, grabbed business wherever it could be found and battled the miserably poor roads in their efforts to survive. Some prospered and grew, others enjoyed modest success—but many are remembered only through faded photos.

Renton-Issaquah (Washington) Auto Freight (Murvin Castagno)

Uses of the motor truck were (and are) virtually endless. In the pioneer era they hauled everything from apples to zucchini squashes, from zinc to asbestos. Body styles were equally numerous; there were flatbeds, low-boys, closed and web-wire panels, pickups, light delivery wagons and massive steel-box ore-carriers. Simply speaking, trucks were for carrying things, and if they didn't come equipped to do the job, the new owners merely re-built them.

Credits (from bottom left clockwise): Sherman Collett, Gayville, South Dakota; Ideal Cement Company; Mrs. V. C. Gilliland, Springfield, South Dakota; U. S. Department of Agriculture; Harrah's Automobile Collection, Reno, Nevada; American Trucking Associations, Inc.; American Trucking Associations, Inc.; Historical Collection, Title Insurance and Trust Company, San Diego; Automobile Manufacturers Association, Inc.

191864

(Opposite page and above) Washington Motor Transport Association

Another domain of the horse was wrested away when trucks moved into logging country. Roads and bridges had to be improved to accommodate the motor vehicles, but in the end great advances were made in speed and efficiency. "Bulldog" Macks were a familiar sight in the tall timber as were dozens of other makes and models.

Trucks in The Tall Timber

WHEN TRUCKS became powerful enough to get off the beaten path, they soon found their way into the woods.

Few assignments tested the strength and durability of a motor vehicle like a season in the tall timber. Load weights were usually as much as the could handle—plus "just a little bit more." The first logging roads ranged from "horribly bad" to "immeasurably worse."

But there were several important reasons why trucks were needed in the forests, and all of them had to do with economics.

When virgin timber stands were unlimited, pioneer loggers used little more than their saws, axes and the forces of nature as they tumbled trees

King County (Washington) Engineer

(Opposite page) Logging was rough and rugged in 1921 when trucks like this picturesque Signal were introduced into the woods. Because of brake failures, runaway vehicles were not uncommon. Note the lack of protection for the driver from sliding logs. (Right) Two old-timers: a study in nostalgia on a Washington State logging road in 1919.

directly into lakes and rivers for eventual floating to mills. In time the distance to the water was great enough to require hauling or skidding. Flumes, chutes and skid roads were built, with oxen employed to apply the brute strength. The doughty beasts played their historical role well, but as demands for lumber increased, they proved too slow and many of them were replaced by horses.

Meanwhile, the great timber companies were developing, and their resources were sufficient enough to permit them to build logging railroads. The latter made it possible to reach deep into the hinterlands where untouched forests were seemingly unending. Again, however, demands were greater than the wildest dreams.

Gradually the trees receded from the rails. In certain ravines and on isolated mountain sides, small tracts of timber were by-passed. Railroads were expensive to build, and they could only go where the production merited them. Shortly before World War I the answer was found in the motor trucks.

Again the sequence was much the same as in highway transport. Animals were slow, inefficient and required too much care. Granted, an oxen which broke a leg could be eaten in the mess hall, but a stack of tough steaks couldn't make up for the drawbacks. Logging trains, on the other hand, were rail-bound, and it was simply unprofitable to extend them into areas offering limited harvest. What's more, locomotives were fire hazards!

So as early as the spring of 1913, a motor truck went to work in the woods near Covington, Washington. Possibly there were earlier applications, but it was in this general period that a new logging technique began to evolve. Trucks did not totally replace animals, nor were they a substitute for the railroads. Instead they played a supplemental role to the latter, extending the radius of operation with less expense.

At first, a great deal of experimentation was necessary. Log trailers were the product of trial and error as truck promoters and timbermen alike worked to perfect a practical system. In time the worst mechanical faults were overcome. Then came the matter of the roads.

As truck logging became more widespread, the

Trucks that were powerful enough for war assignments were equally adaptable to such demanding peace-time pursuits as logging. Garfords, GMCs, Diamond Ts, Macks, Kelly-Springfields, Internationals and other hard-tired behemoths hauled massive loads to mill ponds and cold decks.

Credits (top to bottom): Bill Marenakos; King County (Washington) Engineer; King County (Washington) Engineer; Lansing Division, White Motor Corporation

Special Collections Division, Suzzallo Library, University of Washington

The talents of Photographer Darius Kinsey are well evident in this unusual picture showing a logging truck heading down a steep mountain road. It took extreme courage—or an exaggerated spirit of adventure—to be a teamster under such conditions when brakes weren't altogether dependable, and motors gave out at inopportune times.

(Top) Special Collections Division, Suzzallo Library, University of Washington

(Bottom) Kenworth Motor Truck Company Collection

(Top) A loading boom, a spar tree, a hardy crew and a Diamond T were captured in this photo by Darius Kinsey. The locale was Washington State in the early twenties.

(Bottom) In 1922 there were literally dozens of makes of trucks in the logging industry. This pioneer White represented one of the few names which survived.

Kenworth Motor Truck Company

Built in the center of logging country at Seattle, Washington, Kenworths were ever-present among the tall timbers. It took rugged construction to handle a gargantuan log like the one shown here. Few driving assignments in pioneer trucking days offered the harrowing experiences of piloting a load of fir or cedar down a steep mountainside.

problem of getting in and out of timber tracts grew. Operators began to realize that an investment in a good roadway—still cheaper than a railroad track—would make the use of their vehicles far more efficient . . . and profitable. As a result, three general types of wood-surfaced roads were developed.

The least expensive was called a fore-and-aft pole road. Trees 12 to 14 inches in diameter were hewn flat on at least two sides (as in the drawing at the right). Eight-inch cross-ties were buried in the ground some ten feet apart. They were notched to hold the poles, which were also nailed or bolted to the cross-members for further stability. The poles were buried, too, so that only the flat surface showed. Log guard rails were staked on each side of the road. Trucks, then, were able to travel on two solid wooden tracks.

A fore-and-aft plank road was similar, except that heavy planks—six inches thick and 12 or more inches wide—were used. They were bolted to sunken cross-ties and kept from spreading by blocks and wedges also fastened to the ties. In 1921 such a road cost up to $8,000 a mile, some 25 per cent more than the pole type. The plank roads were extremely effective and permitted loaded trucks to travel 20 miles an hour without

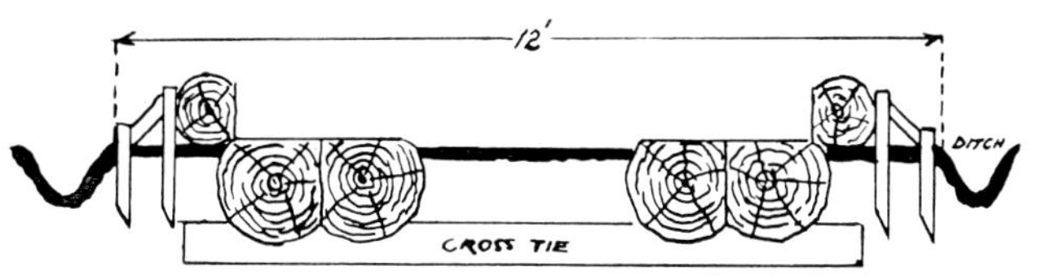

Cross-section of a fore-and-aft pole road used in truck logging operations.

Arthur C. Waller Collection

In the Idaho woods, trucks like this GMC had to be as tough and as hardy as the loggers who used them.

excessive vibration. Traction on these roads was improved by sanding the planks.

The most expensive to build was the cross-plank road. In this case, three rows of poles were imbedded four feet apart running longitudinally with the road bed. Ten-foot planks, six inches thick, were nailed to the protruding surfaces of the poles (see Page 152). To improve traction, the random-width planks were spaced about an inch apart. Because so much planking was required, this type of road was generally limited to short stretches over swampy ground, on steep grades or around sharp curves. The weight of the heavy vehicles continually jarred the nails loose, so maintenance was a worrisome problem. Planks less than six inches thick had a high mortality rate under the massive loads.

Over deep ravines the loggers built trestle bridges, not as elaborate as those for the railroads, but still engineering feats of considerable durability. Along the one-way roads, turn-outs and back-arounds had to be constructed. Crude turntables, made of planks and old circular saws, were used at the ends of some roads. Where the grade was too steep for traction—even with light cables wrapped around the drive wheels—an incline system was provided. This consisted of a mechanical winch called a donkey located at the top of the grade to snub loads down on a cable

(Right) Another spectacular Darius Kinsey photograph preserved for another generation this truck-train of logs. The vehicles were righthand-drive Garfords. Such trestle bridges were known to collapse, adding just one more hazard to the ever-dangerous occupation in the woods. (Below) The Gersix (which eventually became the Kenworth) was built in the logging country of the Pacific Northwest and was therefore designed for heavy loads and axle-snapping terrain.

Kenworth Motor Company Collection

and to haul up empty trucks. Care had to be taken on the downward process to fasten the cable to the load rather than to the truck. That way the logs were under control and couldn't slip forward and crush the driver.

For intermediate grades not quite steep enough to warrant the expense of a donkey, a friction snubber was used. This was nothing more than a cable extending through a system of three or four pulleys. When attached to a truck, the line had enough drag to keep the vehicle from roaring uncontrollably down the hill.

These highlights, of course, simply indicate that truck-logging prior to and immediately after World War I was anything but a joyous Sunday

Special Collection Division, Suzzallo Library, University of Washintgon

outing. It was one of the most dangerous jobs a teamster could ask for. A defective steering system or faulty brakes on a downhill haul could be sheer disaster. Landslides, rickety bridges, sliding logs and other spine-chilling circumstances made the life of a pioneer logging truck driver one harrowing experience after another.

But the motor trucks and their intrepid pilots changed operations in the woods as surely as their counterparts changed highway transportation. They were instrumental in the development of tree-farming. They made it possible to harvest low-grade tracts profitably and to reach isolated areas inaccessible to the railroads. The roads they required opened the forest lands for recreational uses and provided the means for firefighters to reach and battle blazes which otherwise might have raged over thousands of acres without opposition.

Kelly-Springfields, Garfords, GMCs, Diamond Ts, Kenworths, Macks and many other makes saw service in the forested regions of the country. Unlike horses and oxen, they required little care when they weren't on the job. Unfortunately, however, they ultimately eliminated the picturesque bull-puncher whose profane bellowing was a colorful feature of pioneer logging. But on the other hand, a truck driver who threw a tire on a downhill run could fill the air with a few choice words and phrases of his own!

BUILT BY
THE SEAGRAVE COMPANY
COLUMBUS OHIO
...ESER SUPT.
...GRAVE CO.
CHIEF FILLMORE TYSON
LOUISVILLE KY.
CHIEF SAM'L. F. HUNTER
SPRINGFIELD O.
HON. C. A. BURKHARDT
CHIEF FIRE DEPT
ST. BERNARD O.
CHIEF J. F. MERTZ
AKRON O.
C. W. B...
A. G. CRO...
THE S...
...Y ON RETURN FROM 55 MILE RUN FROM
...27TH 1907.

(Opposite page and above) Seattle Fire Department Collection

A 1911 Waterous hose wagon was one of numerous motorized firefighting vehicles which appeared about the same time. The greater proficiency of trucks suddenly made the old horse-drawn gear obsolete, and fire departments throughout the nation began to make the necessary replacements.

Pioneer Days of Motorized Firefighting

IT WAS LOGICAL that with the development of self-propelled vehicles firefighting equipment should be motorized.

As a matter of fact, the replacement of horses for pulling steam pumpers and other equipment was one of the earliest concepts for the use of mechanized carriages.

The first self-driven steam fire engine built in the United States made its appearance in 1840. Paul R. Hodge of New York City designed the clanking monstrosity which proved too slow for practical use. It ended up in a factory as a stationary power plant.

That same year Captain John Ericsson, who

Seattle Fire Department Collection

(Opposite page) One of the earliest motorized firefighters was produced by The Seagrave Company of Columbus, Ohio. This photo was taken in 1907, following a test run of a new truck from Chillicothe to Columbus with the fire chiefs of several cities aboard. (Right) Detroit invested in this Packard squad car before replacing its horse-drawn pumpers.

Seattle Fire Department Collection

A unique Knox three-wheeler with elongated steering apparatus was one of scores of unusual firefighting contraptions introduced in the early 1900s. This unit was owned by the city of Springfield, Massachusetts.

was to become famous for his creation of the iron-clad *Monitor* of the Civil War, won a gold medal for his prototype of a steam firefighter. He claimed to have designed an earlier machine which was built in London in 1829.

But regardless of the originators, steam fire engines — horse-drawn or operated under their own power—found widespread interest. One of the first successful devices was a combination affair built by Moses Latta of Cincinnati in 1852. His steamer—known as the "Joe Ross"—was a three-wheeler pulled by four horses. However, when enough steam was generated, the operator was able to give the horses mechanical assistance. And they needed it! The "Joe Ross" weighed eleven tons, more than some railroad engines of the day.

Incidentally, the crew of Latta's machine was salaried, as the Cincinnati Fire Department also introduced an innovation in personnel. The nation's first paid fire force caused wide consternation among the ranks of the volunteers—in Cincinnati and elsewhere—who feared that motorized equipment and professional crews would wipe out the socio-political system they all favored. But that, of course, is another story!

The Amoskeag Manufacturing Company of Manchester, New Hampshire, was one of the leading pioneer builders of firefighting equipment. As early as 1859 it had steamers on the market; in

The Seattle Fire Department motorized in 1910 with the purchase of two Seagrave hose and ladder units. The Columbus, Ohio, company introduced its first gas pumper the following year.

Seattle Fire Department Collection

Seattle Fire Department Collection

In 1908 the Vancouver, British Columbia, Fire Department boasted this ornately decorated truck which was almost as gaudy as the hats of the ladies posing at the steering wheel. Artistic embellishments were a traditional feature of pioneer firefighting equipment, with even the wheel spokes getting a touch of glamour.

time they were operating successfully from Portland, Maine, to Vancouver, British Columbia. During the great Boston fire of 1872, one of the Amoskeag machines was rushed to the historical city where it helped battle the calamitous blaze which destroyed 767 buildings in less than 24 hours. The city of Boston later bought the steamer.

The excitement of a firefighting unit bursting into action was retained in the motorized era as this photo of an overpopulated squad car readily indicated.

Automobile Manufacturers Association, Inc.

The first motorized fire trucks were self-propelled steamers which dated back to the early 1800s. This ancient vehicle saw service in Vancouver, British Columbia.

Seattle Fire Department Collection

Seattle Fire Department Collection

No parades were complete without units of the local fire department whether motorized or horse-drawn, and sometimes the flame-chasers' band was an added attraction. This picture of Seattle, Washington's musical firefighters was taken in that city's Potlatch parade of 1914 when such giant trucks were becoming more common.

In the same year the LaFrance brothers of Elmira, New York, entered the highly competitive field of fire-equipment manufacturing. Asa LaFrance, a mechanical wizard, turned his talents to a steam pumper which was introduced in 1875. The LaFrance firm, through various mergers and consolidations, ultimately became the American LaFrance Fire Engine Company in 1904 just as the era of the internal combustion engine began its ascendency. The dramatic steam pumper—

In 1914 the city of Minneapolis bought the first FWD fire truck. It was placed in service on September 14, and it worked so well that within two years the Minnesota metropolis had added seven more. The early horse-drawn steam pumpers (like the one being towed by the FWD) required a hot fire to generate the necessary steam. New pumps were operated directly off the truck motors, thus providing a more efficient, self-contained unit.

FWD Corporation

Seattle Fire Department Collection

Following their debut in 1915, "Bulldog" Macks were adapted to every conceivable truck use, including fire-fighting.

Seattle Fire Department Collection

Firefighting equipment was mounted on the chassis of dozens of truck makes before World War I, including the Kelly-Springfield.

which through the years was accused of starting more fires than it put out—was (like the horses which pulled many of them) on its way out. A new concept had emerged!

In St. Paul, Minnesota, the Waterous Fire Engine Works had been experimenting with gas-operated pumps before the turn of the century. In 1898 it introduced a horse-drawn pumper with a small gas engine capable of delivering 300 gallons of water per minute. Engineers of the company—which traced its beginning to Brantford, Ontario, in 1844—kept abreast of automotive developments, and in 1906 they had designed a revolutionary self-propelled, gas-burning pumper. This original Waterous actually had two engines—one to drive the vehicle and the other to operate the pump.

Meanwhile, work continued on the idea of a

By 1910 firemen from coast to coast were posing proudly in new mechanized rigs like this Seagrave. To be sure, there were some skeptics, but by and large, acceptance of self-driven fire engines was widespread.

Washington State Department of Highways

Seattle Fire Department Collection

(Above) A worm-drive Universal, circa 1912, was well ahead of its time in streamlining. Its unusual radiator was a complete departure from the "wagon box" front end of earlier trucks like the 1910 Seagrave (below).

single engine for both truck and pump, and in 1907 Waterous again was the first to succeed. A four-cylinder model was built and delivered to Alameda, California, thus signalling a major change in firefighting equipment. From 1840 to 1907 Waterous again was the first to succeed. A favor—more than 50 companies built some 5,000 of the smoke-spewing devices. The advent of the motor truck made the steamers obsolete, and then the emphasis was shifted to the improvement of the newer horseless fire engines.

Numerous combination vehicles were designed

Seattle Fire Department Collection

Seattle Fire Department Collection

Asa and T. S. LaFrance organized the company bearing their family name in Elmira, New York, in 1872. They introduced their first steam fire engine three years later. In 1904 the American LaFrance Fire Engine Company was formed after a reorganization of the International Fire Engine Company, which itself was a consolidation of several pioneer firms in the same field. American LaFrance made the shift to gas-operated vehicles and continued to be one of the nation's leading producers of fire engines like those above.

and built by an equally numerous list of companies. Knox introduced a chemical car in 1906. The Seagrave Company of Columbus, Ohio—destined to be one of the leading producers of gas-operated fire trucks—was building hose wagons and combination vehicles before coming out with the first centrifugal pumper in 1911. That same year the American LaFrance Company delivered its initial gasoline pumper to San Antonio, Texas; the first Mack pumper went to Phoenixville, Pennsylvania; and the original Robinson piston pumper went into action at Wilmington, Delaware.

Tracing the chronology of firefighting equipment can become a complicated narrative, just as the genealogy of commercial trucks is a mass of intertwined organizations, mergers, short-term successes, unending name-changes and an interminable variety of models, specialty vehicles and innovations. There were, of course, many "mixed" fire engines. The Webb pumper of 1908—first combination hose and pumping apparatus—was actually built on an Oldsmobile chassis. The original Peter Pirsch was a modified White. A Thomas chassis provided the running gear for the first Maxim, while the Howe Fire Apparatus Company used a Model T Ford as its basic unit.

As more and more automotive fire engines were built, an interesting hand-me-down process developed. Equipment was passed from big city to small city to town and hamlet, many units staying in service effectively for a quarter of a century or more, clear proof of the quality of the original products. Unlike most commercial trucks, fire engines received constant care from volunteer and professional firemen. They were not allowed to fall into dis-repair, neither were they overloaded nor over-worked. Longevity was the ultimate result.

Clarence E. Meek, one of the leading historians in the firefighting field, marked 1912 as a milestone year, when steam pumpers came to the end

The Timken Roller Bearing Company

In 1917 this Ahrens-Fox was the pride of the Cincinnati Fire Department. It cost $11,000 when new, and its pumping equipment—mounted ahead of the motor—was capable of delivering 800 gallons per minute.

Historical Collection, Title Insurance and Trust Company, San Diego

By 1915 fire trucks had become massive, powerful vehicles like this Gorham-Seagrave unit which served the city of San Diego. The chain drive and righthand steering had not yet been abandoned, however.

of the road for all intents and purposes. Their gas-powered counterparts—first introduced by Waterous—moved into the forefront, just as gas-driven commercial trucks had doomed steam and electric vans. The Saurer had made its transcontinental run, and the 1912 army road test gave every indication (regardless of what the skeptics said) that a new day was dawning.

(Top) Historical Collection, Title Insurance and Trust Company, San Diego
(Bottom) Union Oil Company of California

Admittedly, it was ten years later before the New York Fire Department retired its last horse-drawn apparatus. Still, 1912 has to go down as a "special" year in the saga of trucks and trucking. From that point on, steam, electricity and *hay* were superseded as prime power sources for commercial transportation and firefighting equipment.

Four Wheel Drive, Nott, Stutz, Moreland, White, Ahrens-Fox, Mack, Peter Pirsch and other manufacturers joined leaders like American LaFrance and Seagrave in the production of vehicles for the nation's fire departments. In the post-war period this list was pared as the struggle for survival carried over to the fire equipment manufacturers.

Many of the same problems which faced other phases of the trucking industry were also present to thwart the mechanized firefighters. Drivers had to be weaned away from horses. Slick, hard-rubber tires spun fruitlessly on dewy cobblestones. Massive motors often defied the muscles attempting to start them with a hand-crank. Somehow, though, the right men were found, the machines got better and the job was accomplished!

(Top left) San Diego's Engine Company No. 1 featured the old and the new, with a motor truck to pull the almost-obsolete steam pumper. (Bottom left) Designed to fight petroleum fires, this unusual truck featured a Rube Goldberg assortment of guages, valves and pipelines.

FWD Corporation

In the mid-twenties the New York City Fire Department purchased 20 FWD tractors like this juggernaut. The same department had replaced its last horse-drawn unit in 1922. Because of the vital demands for power and efficiency, fire trucks often tended to lead the way in terms of mechanical improvements.

Seattle Fire Department Collection

This old steam pumper, pulled by a Seagrave tractor, was still in action in Seattle, Washington, in 1920, long after others like it had been retired. It is shown fighting the disastrous Lincoln Hotel fire of that year.

WE BUY ANNUALLY FROM THE
WASHINGTON FARMERS
For the Manufacture of NATURES GIFT
Rainier PALE BEER
200,000 LBS. HOPS
30,000 000 LBS. of BARLEY

(Opposite page) Sicks' Rainier Brewing Company, Seattle, Washington

Brockway Motor Trucks

The pioneer period of automotive development ended in the mid-twenties. The national road network was gradually being extended and improved, and hundreds of thousands of passenger cars and commercial trucks were on the highways. America was truly "on the move," in every imaginable kind of vehicle, including this early mobile home.

Gadgets, Gimmickry and Gasoline

AMERICA'S FIRST TRUCKS were neither glamorous nor particularly attractive by modern standards. Yet, in their day, they were as aesthetically acceptable as bustles, handlebar mustaches and high button shoes.

They even began to replace horses in parades, although that was one equine stronghold they were never able to overcome.

Functionalism was—and continues to be—the keynote in truck design. In the early days trucks were built, and then often re-built to fit a particular need. Some unusual contraptions resulted, like the mobile home above or the "mechanical giraffe" on Page 174. Many times trucks were really just remodeled cars. After an auto served for a year or two as a passenger-carrier, the rear seat was removed and a box added. Sometimes (as was the case with hundreds of Model Ts) these conver-

(Opposite page) To some degree, trucks even replaced horses in parades—and an American institution, the street-cleaner, faded into history. This Kelly-Springfield was properly adorned for a celebration in Seattle, Washington, in the 1920s. (Right) Trucks—especially Model Ts — were fitted with all sorts of gimmickry to advertise products and services.

Historical Collection, Title Insurance and Trust Company, San Diego

Seattle Post-Intelligencer Library

(Above) The angular lines of pioneer trucks didn't lend themselves to artistic decoration, but when Fourth of July or some other holiday came, the hard-tired trundlers were festooned with balloons and bunting in the spirit of the occasion. (Below) Sometimes the vehicles carried a message—like this coroner's truck and ambulance.

sions would have done Rube Goldberg proud.

The first two decades of the twentieth century were also the era of the open-air sightseeing bus. Ladies in big plumed hats and men with celluloid collars climbed aboard the uncomfortable coaches to gawk at scenery and listen to the megaphone recitals of glib tour directors.

Other promoters took advantage of trucks and autos to create advertising gimmicks for a whole host of products. Self-propelled vehicles attracted attention — especially in outlying hamlets — so drummers plastered them with signs and unique

Seattle Transit System

Circus World Museum, Baraboo, Wisconsin

In 1896 the Barnum & Bailey Circus featured the Duryea Motor-Wagon as a prime attraction. Not many years later autos and trucks became important transportation factors in the movement of traveling shows and carnivals. This restored "Bulldog" Mack was a circus performer following World War I, often replacing elephants instead of horses.

body designs which elicited more gee-whizzes per mile than a clown on a velocipede.

Almost 3,000,000 trucks had been manufactured in the United States by the end of 1925. By that time, however, many of the first ones were dismantled or stored away as relics in barns and warehouses. The evolution of commercial vehicles during that pioneer period was unusually rapid. Amazing progress was made, not only in the trucks themselves, but with the parts and accessories which broadened their use and the fuels and lubricants which made them run.

Wheels and tires, for instance, were a case in point. Flimsy bicycle-type wheels carried some of the first light delivery trucks. In 1888 a Scottish veterinary surgeon, John Boyd Dunlop, had patented an idea for a pneumatic "tyre." This invention greatly increased the interest in cycling and ultimately was vital to the automotive industry. Heavier trucks used wooden carriage or "artil-

Another famous entertainment spectacle of the early decades of the twentieth century was the Miller Brothers 101 Ranch show from Texas. Strictly a Wild West extravaganza, the traveling cowboys-and-Indians circus turned to motor trucks for transportation in its later years. They were more practical than the railroads for one-day stands.

Harrah's Automobile Collection, Reno, Nevada

Historical Collection, Title Insurance and Trust Company, San Diego

In 1911 James J. Jeffries, who had held the world's heavyweight boxing championship from 1899 till 1903, was still very much a celebrity. So too was Berner Eli (Barney) Oldfield, the ex-cycle racer who had become famous as the driver of Henry Ford's tiller-steered "999." The idea of sports favorites endorsing products had already been conceived by the advertising experts, so Jeffries and Oldfield teamed up in this tiny delivery truck to "sell" Nuvida (New Life) Water. Promotion vehicles were widely used for such purposes.

lery" wheels, faced either with steel or hard-rubber. As load weights increased, wooden spokes gave way under the strain, and steel wheels were developed.

Tires—long since taken for granted—offered major problems to early truck and automobile manufacturers. The story of Charles Goodyear's accidental discovery of the vulcanizing process (when he dropped India rubber mixed with white lead and sulphur on a hot stove in 1839) is well known. The adaptation of his product to the running gear of vehicles was anything but happenstance, however. In England Robert W. Thomson patented the forerunner of the modern pneumatic tire in 1845, 43 years before Dunlop's concept was tested on his son's tricycle. By 1881 hansom cabs in London were equipped with solid rubber tires in an effort to reduce the effects of vibration on passengers, lamp brackets and even the exterior varnish. After that, more and more coaches and carriages were similarly fitted.

In the United States Thomas B. Jeffery invented a "clincher" tire for bicycles in 1891. Five years later B. F. Goodrich made the first tires used on a commercial automobile in America. Akron, Ohio, became the world's greatest rubber manufacturing center as The B. F. Goodrich Company was followed by Firestone and Goodyear. The demands of the new automotive industry devoured their production and that of numerous other firms. Rubber importation to the U. S. jumped from 18,000 tons in 1895 to 60,000 tons in 1915.

The inventive mind of man can create some wierd contraptions, and one of these was this adjustable tower mounted on an electric truck. It was adaptable to work on power lines and other lofty assignments. The most unusual feature, however, was the fact that it could be driven and steered at two levels.

Seattle Post-Intelligencer Library

Open-air sightseeing buses were popular favorites in the early 1900s. The Mack brothers' first vehicle, for instance, was a 20-passenger bus built in 1900. Other companies followed with models of various sizes. In addition to their use at fairs—such as the Alaska-Yukon-Pacific Exposition of 1909—the buses were in great demand by resort hotels for shuttling guests back and forth between the railroad stations and the inns.

Until the mid-twenties, most trucks, other than very light models, operated on hard-rubber tires. At first they had smooth surfaces and were vulcanized directly to the wheel rim. In 1903 Henry J. Perlman, son of a Russian-born rabbi, invented a demountable rim so that pneumatic auto tires didn't have to be repaired where flats occurred. This concept was extended to hard-rubber, too, as improvements were continually sought to increase resiliency, traction and longevity. Treads were introduced. At least one manufacturer tried drilling holes through his tires from side to side to give them more "spring." Another filled a hollow casing with the equivalent of modern foam rubber. Contrary to general belief, hard-rubber tires could also "blow out." Bubbles of air between the rubber and the rim or metal base would expand due to heat and friction. The result would be an explosion strong enough to rip out a considerable section of tire—and the hapless truck

Seattle Historical Society

With a megaphone and an appropriate line of chatter, the sightseeing conductor kept his customers entertained and informed. The buses were often crude and cantankerous, but at the time, no one seemed to mind.

Zack Benn of Anacortes, Washington, probably owned the nation's first motor-driven lunch stand. Built in 1912 with a Model T Ford for power, it was a popular vehicle at fairs, picnics and carnivals in the Pacific Northwest. In an era of innovation, entrepreneurs had new fields to conquer with the advent of autos and motor trucks. Imagination was the only limiting factor as commercial visionaries began to develop a great variety of mobile shops. A new kind of "drummer"—with his wares in his own truck—clattered down the backroads to make his calls on farmers and farm wives.

The Seattle Times

involved would clunk down the road, "limping" each time the blank section came around.

Lighting was another major problem in the early days of trucking. At first, feeble kerosene lamps were used, although night-time driving under such conditions was avoided as much as possible. In 1904 Carl Graham Fisher and James A. Allison organized the Prest-O-Lite Company to perfect a system using acetylene gas. For years, a Prest-O-Lite tank was a familiar addition to most trucks. By 1912 the first electric headlights were coming into use, and three years later prism lenses were introduced to extend the beams. It was a step-by-step process, though, as some ideas were tried and discarded, while others were successful and gained wide acceptance.

Facile minds continued to tackle a wide range of automotive deficiencies. As early as 1903 a heavy-duty Columbia Electric truck featured a power-steering unit operating off a separate electric motor. Autocar introduced a seat-over-engine model with shaft-driven axle in 1907. A year later Otto Zachow and William Besserdich unveiled their four-wheel-drive "Battleship." In 1909 Gramm trucks sported overdrive transmissions. It was a continuing struggle to develop newer and better devices and systems. In 1912 Charles F. Kettering of the Dayton Engineering Laboratories Company (Delco) completed work on an electric starter which was adopted by Cadillac. Almost concurrently, Prest-O-Lite introduced an acetylene starter. The National Automobile Show that year featured a Sampson truck with a compressed-air dump body and a Pope-Hartford with a tilting cab for access to the motor located under the seat.

Meanwhile, another developmental process was underway.

As gasoline-operated vehicles grew in favor, fuel demands leaped proportionately. "Gasolene"

(Top) Standard Oil Company of California
(Botom) Earle G. Shettleworth, Jr., Collection, Maine Historical Society

(Top right) It was moving day on the oilfields, so this wooden-wheeled Packard picked up a shack and toted it to a new location. (Bottom right) Imaginative promoters, such as this baker in Portland, Maine, used gimmickry to sell their products.

The Seattle Times

In 1907 John McLean, a representative of the Standard Oil Company of California, reputedly opened the first service station in America. It was located in Seattle, Washington, and consisted of an old hot-water tank and a hose under a rough wooden canopy. Gas was delivered by gravity. McLean's idea gradually spread, but for a long time motorists and truck drivers filled up at apothecaries, general stores, lumberyards, blacksmith shops and even livery stables where petroleum products were carried as a sideline.

or "stove naphtha" was originally a by-product of the distillation of kerosene, which in 1900 was the petroleum industry's biggest seller. Gas molecules were the first to boil off of the crude oil in the distillation process, and since it was virtually a waste material, manufacturers made sure none of the valuable kerosene would be mixed with it. Consequently, the gasoline at the turn of the century was amazingly high in octane. Later when kerosene became the secondary product, its larger molecules were permitted to enter the gas, thus reducing its combustion qualities. This was true of both the distillation and "cracking" processes, the latter being developed by Dr. William M. Burton in 1913.

So, for a time, instead of getting better, gasoline got worse. The infamous motor knock became a factor to deal with; the problem was the delayed firing of larger molecules. Thomas Midgley and Charles Franklin Kettering experimented endlessly in search of a solution. They discovered that iodine would work, but it was too expensive. Aniline was also effective — but odoriferous. Tetraethyl lead ultimately answered all the requirements, and the first Ethyl went on the market in 1923.

By then, service stations and garages were becoming commonplace. Before that, gasoline was purchased at lumber yards, livery stables, apothecaries, general stores and right off the back of delivery wagons. A five-gallon can with a potato jammed on the spout was a constant companion of the pioneer trucker.

Altogether, these processes of industrial evolution added up to the modern truck. The nostalgic past promised an exciting future!

In the Hawaiian Islands the Wailuku Auto Supply Company put its service station on wheels, delivering gas directly from this Model T Ford. It was not an easy matter to keep the burgeoning numbers of trucks and cars operating in the pioneer days when supplies were limited and facilities almost non-existent.

Standard Oil Company of California

Historical Collection, Title Insurance and Trust Company, San Diego

For a time horses and motor trucks shared the city streets —and then the horses were gone. The change, though resisted by a persistent few, was inevitable!

A Final Word...

THE MOST GRATIFYING aspect of a backward glance is that it permits you to see how far you've come!

In the span of a single lifetime, the trucking industry was born, floundered through its early years and then matured in a continuing wave of technological and administrative advances.

Modern highway juggernauts are the great-grandchildren of spindly delivery vans which made their appearance in the late 1890s. Ungainly as they were, they heralded the end of the centuries-old horse-based system of transportation. Some 100 years earlier, James Watt had experimented in England with heavy draft animals and established that one "horsepower" is equal to 746 watts of electrical energy or the rate of "pull" necessary to raise 33,000 pounds one foot per minute. In less than three decades after the introduction of the motor truck, Old Dobbin was relegated to the pasture, and horsepower—as far as commercial transport was concerned—came almost exclusively on wheels.

By historical standards, the shift from horse-drawn vehicles to automotive conveyances was virtually an "over-night" phenomenon. Almost three million trucks were operating on American roadways in 1925—and neither the trucks nor the roads had scarcely been envisioned a short quarter of a century earlier.

The significance of this transportation revolution has now become obvious. The entire socio-economic structure of the United States was changed. Since the Cruickshank Engineering Works of Providence, Rhode Island, converted a horse van into a steam wagon to haul furniture for the Shepard & Company department store of that city in 1896, the transformation has been relentless.

Of course, there were feeble efforts to resist the inevitable.

A few early drivers and their vehicles were

By the mid-twenties there was no turning back the calendar: the automotive age had truly arrived! Growing fleets of trucks like this had to be assembled to deliver the petroleum products demanded by the motorists of America.

stoned and otherwise physically abused. The derisive cry, "Get a Horse," was often seriously intended. Worried teamsters—fearful for their jobs—threw sand in the batteries of electric trucks and resorted to sabotage of one type or another. In 1895 Chicago had an ordinance banning horseless carriages from city streets. Other scattered attempts were made to legislate against autos and trucks, but in the end the march of science and progress could be no more than momentarily detoured.

The earliest motor trucks are now historical relics. Some of them have been preserved for future generations to view and contemplate. And that, too, is why this book was written: to help maintain a link with the pioneer trucks and truckers who accomplished more than they could ever have imagined!

White Motor Corporation

In 1915 a White truck was selected to haul the Liberty Bell to the railroad station when it was shipped from Philadelphia to the Panama-Pacific Exposition in San Francisco.

Standard Oil Company of California

Suzzallo Library, University of Washington

This ruggedly constructed Kelly-Springfield was typical of the pioneer motor trucks which brought a technological change to the logging industry shortly before World War I.

Elsewhere trucks of all shapes and sizes were revolutionizing scores of other businesses, replacing horses and supplementing the railroads.

Arthur W. Lee Collection

Arthur W. Lee (right) and George V. Eastes (center) began operating their own truck line in 1923 between Seattle and Puyallup, Washington, with a single Service truck. Two years later they had this fleet of four: a White, a Dodge and two Macks. Ultimately Lee & Eastes, Inc., became one of the West Coast's major carriers. The company's development was typical of one-truck operations which grew with the general expansion of the industry.

The Language of the Truck Driver

Every occupation has its own lexicon—words and phrases which have special meanings to those who are involved. Truck drivers are no exception. Almost since the first electric and steam delivery vans appeared on big city streets, a "teamster's terminology" has been developing. Some expressions are of pioneer vintage; others are products of a later date. Here is a sampling of the more unusual figures of speech long used by truckers:

Armstrong starter: Hand crank.

Balloon freight: Light, bulky cargo.

Barbwire drive: Chain-drive.

Bareback: Tractor without its semi-trailer.

Battery acid: A cup of coffee at the truck stop.

Bean hauler: A driver who transports fruits and vegetables.

Bobtail: Same as bareback; also a straight truck.

Brownie: Auxiliary transmission.

Bull hauler: One who hauls livestock.

Button her up: Tie down the load on a truck or trailer.

Crackle crate: Truck hauling live poultry.

Cement mixer: Truck with a noisy engine or transmission.

City shag: City delivery.

Cowboy: Reckless driver.

Cradle: Battery compartment on electric truck.

Dock-walloper: One who handles freight across a dock, and who loads and unloads vehicles.

Dog: Truck with little power.

Drag down: Shift down to lower gears too slowly.

Drop it on the nose: Accidentally pulling a tractor out from under a semi-trailer.

Dusting: Vehicle riding with one wheel off of the pavement and throwing up a cloud of dust.

Four-banger: Four cylinder engine.

Garbage wagon: Produce truck.

Goose it: Feed gasoline to an engine in irregular spurts or suddenly race the engine.

Grandma: Lowest gear.

Grinding a pound: Incorrect meshing of gears.

Gypsy: An independent truck operator who drives his own truck and secures freight wherever he can.

Hauling post-holes: Driving an empty truck or trailer.

High binder: Truck driver with racing tendencies.

Homing Pigeon: An electric truck which had to get back to the barn before its power gave out.

Horse: Tractor or power unit.

Hot load: Emergency shipment of cargo needed in a hurry.

Hundred mile coffee: Coffee strong enough to keep you wide awake for at least 100 miles.

Kick down: Shift down to lower gear.

Kidney buster: Hard-riding truck.

Load her heavy on the high side: Load toward left side of trailer so as to be heavier on the higher side of the road.

Mexican overdrive: No brakes.

Peach picker: A very high cab-over-engine truck.

Peanut wagon: Small truck pulling a large trailer.

Peddle run: Truck run with frequent deliveries enroute.

Rag top: Open-top trailer using a tarpaulin for covering.

Rags: Tires.

Semi (Pronounced sem-eye): Semi-trailer.

Shaking hands with the sticks: Shifting gears with both hands.

Sick horse: A truck in poor mechanical condition, especially with low power.

Six-banger: Six-cylinder engine.

Skins: Tires.

Sled: Trailer which pulls hard.

Snub nose: Engine under cab.

Stem winder: Hand-crank starter.

Straight job: A truck which has a body built onto its chassis.

Swamper: Same as dock-walloper; also a helper riding in the truck.

Tailgating: Riding too closely behind the vehicle ahead.

Tractor: Truck used to pull semi-trailers.

Yard mule: Small tractor used to move semi-trailers around the terminal yard.

Electric trucks ran until their batteries petered out. Consequently, their work assignments had to be organized so that they'd be back in the "barn" before they ran out of power. In truckers' lingo, therefore, they were called "homing pigeons."

Seattle Historical Society

Kenworth Motor Truck Company Collection

Haulin' Pete

"His Brains Are in His Feet"

Haulin' Pete was a merry old soul,
  A merry old soul was he.
He hauled by the ton;
He hauled by the peck;
  Or he hauled for a lousy fee.

He weren't particular 'bout what he drug,
  Or where he drug it to.
A load of spuds,
Or someone's duds—
  He'd haul for a song or two.

He'd sit on the top of a hefty load
  And sing till he bust a tire.
His truck was the bunk,
A mess o' junk—
  He was merely a hauler for hire!

Anonymous*

---

*From **Western Truck Owner,** predecessor of **Western Trucking Magazine**, October, 1926.

Special Collections Division, Suzzallo Library, University of Washington

The Diamond T was a popular work-horse in the forests of the Pacific Northwest. This fleet of pioneer logging vehicles was lined up for the benefit of Photographer Darius Kinsey on Camano Island, Washington State, in 1920. Such rigs were stripped down for functionalism; rugged construction was mandatory.

Earl Staley Collection

Automatic dump trucks revolutionized the materials hauling industry and made the age-old shovel just a little less important. Hand-loaded wagons simply couldn't compete with motorized equipment.

Bibliography

Anderson, Rudolph E. *The Story of the American Automobile.* Washington, D. C.: Public Affairs Press, 1950.

Automobile Manufacturers Association. *A Chronicle of the Automotive Industry in America 1893-1949.* Detroit: 1949.

———. *Automobiles of America.* Detroit: Wayne State University Press, 1962.

Babcock, Irving B. *20 Years' Progress in Commercial Motor Vehicles.* Detroit: Denham and Company for the Automotive Council for War Production, 1942.

Clymer, Floyd. *Motor Scrapbooks.* Numbers 1 through 6, Los Angeles: 1944-50.

———. *Those Wonderful Old Automobiles.* New York: Bonanza Books, Crown Publishers, Inc., 1953.

———. *Treasury of Early American Automobiles.* New York, Toronto, London: McGraw-Hill Book Company, Inc., 1950.

Cornwell, E. L. *Commercial Road Vehicles.* London: B. T. Batsford, 1960.

Donovan, Frank. *Wheels for a Nation.* New York: Thomas Y. Crowell Company, 1965.

Glasscock, C. B. *The Gasoline Age.* New York: The Bobbs-Merrill Co., 1937.

Homans, James E. *Self-Propelled Vehicles.* New York: Theo. Audel & Company, 1908.

Knapp, Frederick M. *Motor Truck Logging Methods.* Seattle, Washington: University of Washington Engineering Experiment Station Bulletin, 1921.

La Schum, Edward E. *The Electric Motor Truck.* New York: U.P.C. Book Company, Inc., 1924.

Lewis, Eugene W. *Motor Memories.* Detroit: Alved, Publishers, 1947.

Lief, Alfred. *The Firestone Story.* New York, Toronto, London: McGraw-Hill Book Company, Inc., 1951.

Meek, Clarence E. "From Hand Cranks to Self-Starters," *Fire Engineering* (Lancaster, Pa.), Vol. 113, Numbers 8 and 9 (August, September, 1960).

Musselman, M. M., *Get a Horse.* Philadelphia-New York: J. B. Lippincott Company, 1950.

Pound, Arthur. *The Turning Wheel.* New York: Doubleday, Doran & Company, 1934.

Rae, John B. *American Automobile Manufacturers.* Philadelphia: Chilton Company, 1959.

Rolt, L. T. C. *Horseless Carriage.* London: Constable and Company, Ltd., 1950.

Sibley, Hi. *Merry Old Mobiles on Parade.* Garden City, N. Y.: Garden City Books, 1951.

Troyer, Howard William. *The Four Wheel Drive Story.* New York, Toronto, London: McGraw-Hill Book Company, Inc., 1954.

White Motor Corporation. *The Albatross. A Quarter Century of White Transportation.* Cleveland: 1925.

Refueling of a vintage airplane in Fairbanks, Alaska, was a crowd-luring spectacle in the early 1920s. A Model T Ford—a spectacle itself a few years before—drew little attention as it played its work-horse role.

Standard Oil Company of California

Frederick & Nelson, Seattle, Washington

Department stores from coast to coast ranked among the earliest users of trucks for delivery purposes. In Seattle, Washington, Frederick & Nelson replaced horses with the fleet shown above. The four trucks on the right had celluloid windshields which could be rolled up when the weather was good.

Index

General

People

It was not unusual for a company like Seattle City Light to have a hodge-podge fleet of assorted makes in the pioneer days of trucking. The mortality rate of models was extremely high on the battlefield of competition.

Seattle Historical Society

Pennsylvania Historical and Museum Commission, Harrisburg

As soon as inter-city freighting became feasible, means were sought to increase loads and reduce expenses. Trailers were an obvious development. The first ones were as crude as the earliest trucks, but improvement was rapid and innovations were many. The model above, for instance, had an adjustable body length. Meanwhile, August Fruehauf and his associates in Detroit were creating a wide range of semis, two of which are pictured below.

Places

Fruehauf Corporation

Fruehauf Corporation

Sicks' Rainier Brewing Company, Seattle, Washington

Sentimentally, it was difficult for breweries to shift from their beautiful matched teams of Percherons and Clydesdales—but economically the handwriting was clearly etched on the stable walls. Early trucks were anything but works of art (as the fleet above shows), but in time the designers began to consider over-all appearance.

Trucks

Kenworth Motor Truck Company

Western Trucking Magazine

The profile of the "Bulldog" Mack ranked with that of Andy Gump for quick recognition by truckers and laymen alike. Lined up for inspection in Los Angeles was the original fleet of the Asbury Truck Company in 1922.

The Seattle Times

Jack Fortune (second from left) had little idea he was creating a trucking company when he bought his first horse and wagon in 1903. To the Seattle waterfront he hauled pigtail-wearing Chinese, bound for the fish canneries of Alaska. He carted salmon to the fish markets and gold bullion to the bank vaults. His business prospered, and by 1916—when the above picture was taken—he had switched from horses to his first trucks (North Westerns).

Colophon

Engravings for this book were made by Artcraft Engraving and Electrotype Company, Seattle. It was printed in the same city by Frayn Printing Company. Vintage headline type came from the collection of William O. Thorniley. The paper is Consolidated Paper Company's Production Gloss, supplied by West Coast Paper Company, Seattle. The book was bound by Lincoln and Allen, Portland, Oregon.